A PRIMER ON INTELLECTUAL PROPERTY LICENSING

Second Edition

By Heather J. Meeker

ISBN: 1-58749-463-9

All rights reserved

© 2001, 2004

Earthling Press ~ United States of America

A Primer on Intellectual Property Licensing by Heather J. Meeker
Copyright 2001, 2003 by Heather J. Meeker

Print edition 2003 (Second Edition)
Isbn: 1-58749-463-9
Electronic edition 2001 (First Edition)
Isbn: 1-18749-103-6
All trade paperback and electronic rights reserved

Printed in the United States of America. No part of this book may be used or reproduced without written permission, except in the case of brief quotations embodied in reviews or articles. For more information address the publisher at www.awe-struck.net.

Published by Earthling Press
A subsidiary of Awe-Struck E-Books, Inc.
Printed in the United States of America

www.awe-struck.net

Available in electronic and print formats

Editors Kathryn Struck, Dick Claassen, and Mary Taffs
Cover art by: Cathi Stevenson

TABLE OF CONTENTS

I.	**INTRODUCTION**	1
II.	**WEEK 1: WHY LICENSE?—ANATOMY OF A SHRINK-WRAP LICENSE**	3
III.	**WEEK 2: CONTRACT BASICS AND DRAFTING STYLE**	11
	Basics of contract drafting	*11*
	Verbs and Other Language in Contract Drafting	*13*
	Verbs	*13*
	Other Language in Contract Drafting	*16*
IV.	**WEEK 3: THE UNIVERSE OF DEALS**	21
	Software Distribution Agreements	*23*
	Who Makes Copies?—Resellers versus Publishers	*24*
	Whose Brand?—Resellers versus OEMs	*25*
	Variations on a Theme—VARs	*26*
	Who Takes Title?—Resellers versus Sales Representatives	*26*
	All Other Manner of Creature —Distributors versus Nondescript Species	*27*
	Arrangement	*27*
	Flow of Rights, Flow of Goods	*28*
V.	**WEEK 4: PRIVITY AND INTEGRATION**	31
	Three Party Agreements	*31*
	Confidentiality	*32*
	When is a corporation not a corporation? Divisions and Departments.	*33*
	Non-Competition Covenants	*33*
	Third Parties and Purchase Agreements	*35*
	Flow-Down Provisions	*35*
	Integration	*38*
VI.	**WEEK 5: OWNERSHIP AND TRANSFER OF INTELLECTUAL PROPERTY**	41
	Things Are Not Ideas.	*41*
	Enabling Rights	*42*
	How and When Ownership Arises	*43*
	"Work For Hire": How does a corporation come to own intellectual property?	*43*
	Joint Authorship: The Road Down the Garden Path	*45*
	Who Will Own Intellectual Property?	*46*
	How to Assign Intellectual Property	*47*
	Quitclaim Grants	*48*
	The Transfer of Trademarks	*48*
VII.	**WEEK 6: LICENSE GRANTS**	51
	Exclusivity	*51*
	Territory	*52*
	Term and Royalty	*53*
	Scope and Field of Use	*54*
	Drafting License Grants	*55*
	Trademark licenses	*57*
VIII.	**WEEK 7: CONFIDENTIALITY AND NON-DISCLOSURE**	63
	Doing Deals in the Web Space—Use and "Ownership" of Data	*65*
	Non-Disclosure Agreement Checklist	*68*
IX.	**WEEK 8: ROYALTIES**	71
	Drafting Payment Provisions	*71*
	Avoiding Antitrust Violations	*73*
	Patent Royalties	*74*
	Revenue Recognition	*75*
	Payment Terms and INCOTERMS	*76*

X.	**WEEK 9: BANKRUPTCY AND ESCROWS**	**79**
	Continuation of Rights	*79*
	Bankruptcy Law Summary	*80*
	Section 365(n)	*81*
	Escrows: Access to Source Code and Technology	*81*
	The Flow-Down Problem	*84*
XI.	**WEEK 10: SELECTED TOPICS ON INTERNATIONAL LICENSING**	**87**
	Distributors and Sales Agents	*87*
	Antitrust and the E.U.	*88*
	Differences in Intellectual Property Law	*88*
	Withholding Tax	*89*
	Dispute Resolution and Selection of Governing Law	*89*
	Export Restrictions	*90*
	Language Clauses	*91*
XII.	**WEEK 11: WARRANTIES, INDEMNITIES AND LIMITATIONS OF LIABILITY**	**93**
	Warranty	*93*
	Indemnities	*94*
	Limitations of Liability	*96*
	Warranty Disclaimers	*98*
	Advanced Topic—Intellectual Property Warranties	*99*
XIII.	**WEEK 12: ETHICS AND NEGOTIATION**	**109**
	Professional Rules	*109*
	How to Conduct a Negotiation	*110*
	The Unwritten Rules of Custom and Professional Courtesy	*110*
	Negotiation Tips	*111*
	Indemnity Proposed by Licensor	*113*
	Indemnity Proposed by Licensee	*113*
XIV.	**WEEK 13: SUBSTANTIVE REVIEW: MISC. CONTRACT LAW**	**115**
	Choice of Law and Venue	*115*
	Alternative Dispute Resolution	*118*
	Assignment	*119*
	Other Provisions	*121*
	Notices	*121*
	Waiver	*121*
	Integration or "Entire Agreement"	*122*
	Severability	*122*
XV.	**HYPOTHETICALS**	**125**
XVI.	**APPENDIX—SAMPLE EXAM QUESTIONS**	**127**
XVII.	**APPENDIX—FORM AGREEMENTS**	**131**
XVIII.	**FORM 1: "SHRINK WRAP" TYPE END USER LICENSE**	**133**
XIX.	**FORM 2: "OEM" SOFTWARE DISTRIBUTION AGREEMENT**	**137**
XX.	**FORM 3: MARKETING AND DISTRIBUTION AGREEMENT**	**143**
XXI.	**FORM 4: "CO-BRANDING" AGREEMENT**	**151**

I. Introduction

Several years ago, I began teaching a seminar at Hastings College of the Law (University of California at San Francisco) in technology and intellectual property licensing. I began looking for a textbook to use in the course, but I could not find one. Useful practice-related materials were difficult to find, and many were outdated. So I began preparing material for a course reader. This text is the result of that work.

This text is intended to be used as a course book for my seminar. However, many lawyers in practice have asked me what materials they can read to learn intellectual property licensing, so I have written this book also with a view to providing what I hope will be useful advice for practicing attorneys who are new to the area of intellectual property licensing.

This text assumes that the reader has a basic knowledge of both contract law and intellectual property law. In the area of contract law, the most important things to know for the transactional practice are rules of contract interpretation. These are summarized in the text. Intellectual property law is a broad area consisting mostly of the law of patents, copyrights, trade secrets, and trademarks. Basic intellectual property concepts are summarized in the chapter on writing license grants. There are other areas of law that bear upon the licensing practice: antitrust, unfair competition, employment, tax, and bankruptcy, but you need not know any of these areas in depth to use this text.

This text represents a viewpoint on the practice of licensing that is not be shared by all, so I should explain how my viewpoint was shaped by my practice. My practice is limited to the field of technology transactions, a large part of which is intellectual property licensing. Intellectual property transactions are more than simply licenses—they are business agreements. They often contain licenses of intellectual property, because technology companies that do business together often need to use each other's technology, and this is accomplished through intellectual property licenses.

The viewpoint I mention above has mostly to do with the kind of drafting style and practice I use, both in this book and in my work. This style is based on the following ideas:

- Get the business deal right. All else is secondary.
- Don't over-lawyer any deal or you will kill it.
- Your clients should be able to understand the agreements they are signing.

Some lawyers will disagree with this style and outlook. I feel that this style has been necessitated by my practice. I specialize in representing technology startup clients. Most startup companies—at least at the outset of my representation—have little staff, no legal staff, and few resources. They need to sign transactional agreements quickly to book revenue, get financing, or attract press attention. Their principal aim is not to eliminate risk from an agreement—an aim more typical of larger companies that are "deep pockets" and easy targets for litigation. Lawyers who represent startups are, in large part, business advisors. We are called upon to structure business deals and recommend what risks our clients should take—not to act as scribes and be sure that all risks are eliminated. When we are asked to identify risks, we need to make practical decisions about them, because our clients often have more experience in technology development than in business, and they rely on us to tell them what risks are worst, and what risks—even the bad ones—are simply facts of business life for business people in their position.

Finally, my practice has centered on software clients. In practical terms, this means that the examples I give will focus on this field. This might be different from some readers' expectations in the sense that I do not focus on patent licensing, and I do not focus on traditional content licensing such as that practiced in the entertainment industry. I believe, however, that software licensing is a good baseline, because it is complex enough to invoke most of the most important issues in the licensing practice. The principles in this book can handily be applied to those fields as well, but custom and practice will vary from the examples I present in this book. Also, while most attorneys in my practice do some mergers and acquisitions work, this book is not focused on that practice. However, some of the practice tips in this book are intended to help avoid problems in the merger and acquisition transactions that are likely to be the "liquidity events" or "exit strategies" (i.e. the way the investors get their money out of the business) for start-up clients.

I hope you find this text useful. I welcome your comments and suggestions, which you may send to me at hmeeker@heathermeeker.com. If you send a comment or question, please let me know the edition you are using (This is edition 1.2.), and whether you are a student or a practicing attorney (and if the latter, your firm and practice area).

Heather Meeker, Boalt '94

Oakland, California, 2003

The materials in this text have been prepared by Heather Meeker for informational purposes only, are not legal advice and should not be relied on as legal advice. This text is not intended to substitute for obtaining legal advice from competent, independent, legal counsel in the relevant jurisdiction. Your use of this text is not intended to create and does not constitute a lawyer-client relationship.

II. Week 1: Why License?—Anatomy of a Shrink-Wrap License

If we wish to undertake the task of learning the practice of technology licensing, we should step back for a moment to ask why we write licenses. The drafting of license agreements is a time-consuming and expensive prospect for clients, and it is important to understand why it is necessary, given the broad background of intellectual property law in the United States. To answer this question, we will examine the provisions of a typical "shrink-wrap" end user license (such as Form I in Appendix) and ask the question: Why do we license software?

Here is why the question needs to be asked. If you walk into a bookstore, looking for a copy of the latest bestseller, you select your book, take it to the cash register, pay for it, and are never asked to enter into a license agreement to use the book. Alternatively, if you buy a copy of a spreadsheet application program from the same store, you pay for the software, and when you load the CD-ROM into your computer the first time, you are asked to agree to the terms of a software license agreement to use your copy of the spreadsheet program. Why are the business practices different for these two products? Each is a single copy of a copyrightable work. The book, like the software, is a work of authorship and subject to copyright laws. Purchasing a copy of a book or a copy of a software product entitles you to use that copy, and little else. Your purchase does not give you the right to make further copies, distribute those copies, perform the work in a public place, or exercise any of the other rights of copyright. So, why are you required to enter into a license agreement for the software and not the book? Does the law apply differently to books and software? Is a license necessary?

With this question in mind, we turn to the provisions of a typical shrink-wrap license agreement. The first paragraph of a shrink-wrap license agreement explains how you manifest assent to the terms of the agreement. It states: "By filling in the user information and clicking the button marked 'I ACCEPT' below, you agree to be bound by the terms of this Agreement." There is no need to discuss this provision at length for the purposes of our question. This preamble merely clarifies that you manifest assent to the terms of the agreement by clicking a button rather than by signing your name.

The first substantive provision of the agreement, the "Grant of License," states:

> This Agreement permits use of one copy of the specified version of the Software...on only one computer, and only by one user, at a time.

As we go through the rest of the agreement, we should consider whether, if you bought a copy of the software with no written agreement, you would have the right to do any more than this. The provision further states:

> The Software is "in use" on the computer when it is loaded into temporary memory (i.e., RAM) or installed into permanent memory (e.g., hard disk, CD-ROM or other storage device) of that computer.

Now let us turn to 17 U.S.C. § 117. It states:

> It is not an infringement for the owner of a copy of a computer program to make or authorize the making of another copy or adaptation of that computer program provided: (i) that such a new copy or adaptation is created as an essential step in the utilization of the computer program in conjunction with a machine or that it is used in no other manner, or (ii) that such new copy or adaptation is for archival purposes only and that all archival copies are destroyed in the event that continued possession of the computer program should cease to be rightful.

The provisions of Section 117 and the grant of license here look suspiciously similar. Note that the next section of the license under "Copyright" allows the user to make one copy of the software "solely for back-up or archival purposes." As the "owner of a copy" of the software, you can exercise certain rights of copyright. If you were to ask a lawyer to name any significant substantive difference between the rights granted under this license and the rights that would be available to the purchaser of a copy of a computer program under default copyright law, the answer might be a resounding silence. In any case, it seems that the extent of the difference would not justify the expense and difficulty of drafting and implementing a shrink-wrap license agreement.

The next section, "Copyright," states that the software is "owned by Company or its suppliers or its licensors and is protected by United States copyright laws and international treaty provisions." Clearly, an agreement is not necessary to make a work of authorship subject to copyright law. The copyright rights in the software vested automatically long before this agreement was prepared.

The next section of the agreement, "Restrictions," states:

> You may not rent, lease, or loan the Software.

The section called "Restrictions" further states:

> You may transfer your rights under this Agreement permanently, provided you transfer this Agreement, the Software and all accompanying printed materials, retain no copies, and the recipient agrees to the terms of this Agreement.

Take a look now at 17 U.S.C., § 109(a), otherwise known as the "First Sale Doctrine."

> [T]he owner of a particular copy or phonorecord lawfully made under this title...is entitled, without the authority of the copyright owner, to sell or otherwise dispose of the possession of that copy.

In other words, after the first time a copy of a work of authorship is sold, the distribution right vested in the author is exhausted. So, if you buy a copy of a book, videotape or software CD, you may turn around and sell that copy to another person, provided you convey to him all of the materials in your possession that you received when you bought the product.

Take a look at Section 17 U.S.C. § 109, otherwise known as the "Computer Software Rental Act." Subsection (b)(1)(A) states:

> [T]he owner of a particular...copy of a computer program, may [not], for the purposes of direct or indirect commercial advantage, dispose of, or authorize the disposal of, the possession of that...computer program...by rental, lease or lending...

The copyright law of the United States does not allow the owner of a copy of software to rent or loan the copy to others for commercial purposes. This is in contrast to the rights in the owner of a book or videotape, for instance, and this is why libraries and videotape rental stores are familiar, whereas software rental stores are non-existent.

The last portion of the "Restrictions" section, however, does contain some language that is not consistent with default copyright law. It states: "You may not reverse engineer, decompile or disassemble the Software, except to the extent the foregoing restriction is expressly prohibited by applicable law."

Case law in the United States allows a person who possesses a lawful copy of a piece of software to make copies of it for the purposes of reverse engineering in certain limited situations, such as to make the software compatible with other technology for the user's own purposes. However, this agreement attempts to prohibit by contract what has been allowed under United States case law. Thus, this is one of the substantive differences between default law and the terms of the agreement.

Finally, the "Restrictions" section states that the user may not modify or create derivative works based on the software, but as you can see in 17 U.S.C. § 106, the right to prepare derivative works is one of the exclusive rights of copyright, and a user would be prohibited from exercising that right without a license in any event; in other words, the purchase of a copy does not by implication grant a license to prepare derivative works. Again, there is no difference worth hiring a lawyer to write an agreement.

The next provision of this agreement is the "Limited Warranty." Note that under this limited warranty, which is customary in end user license agreements, the licensor warrants only that the media on which the software is furnished will be free from defects for a period of 90 days. From a business perspective, this is a very limited warranty indeed. It says nothing about the operation of the software. The agreement further states that the only remedy for this warranty is replacement of media.

Most of the law concerning warranties and in consumer software license agreements comes from the Uniform Commercial Code (or UCC) and relevant consumer protection law. Limited warranties are enforceable under the UCC if the limitations are set forth conspicuously. Exclusive remedies are allowed under UCC § 2-719. Note that the language at the end of this section:

This warranty gives you specific legal rights. You may have others that vary from state to state.

This language is required by the Magnusson-Moss Warranty Act.

The next section of this agreement disclaims all warranties other than the ones explicitly set forth in the previous paragraph.

The UCC is a set of uniform state laws that have been adopted by every state in the United States with little variation. The Uniform Commercial Code, Article 2, applies to the sale of goods. Under the UCC, software is considered a good and a license is considered a sale. All sales of goods covered by the UCC are subject to several implied warranties, in other words, those warranties arise in favor of the purchaser whether or not the sales contract expresses them. Those warranties are merchantability, fitness for a particular purpose, and title.

However, the UCC allows a licensor to disclaim these warranties if the disclaimer is conspicuous under UCC § 2-316. Warranties of merchantability and fitness for a particular purpose can give rise to significant damages for a merchant. For instance, with respect to a hard good such as a cup, merchantability might mean that it does not break immediately or that it holds liquid. However, with respect to software, the idea of merchantability is more difficult to grasp. Does it mean the software is error free? This is unlikely, because no software is error free. However, licensors do not wish to explore the interpretation of merchantability of software at the expense of high legal bills, preferring instead to disclaim warranties of merchantability under their license agreements. Thus, the disclaimer of warranties is a significant purpose of an end user license agreement, and is a significant departure from default law.

The UCC provides that with respect to licenses of intellectual property, the warranty of title is a warranty of non-infringement. (See UCC § 2-312.) Finally, note that the language at the end of this section, "Some states do not allow limitations on implied warranties, so the above limitation may not apply to you," is also required by the Magnusson-Moss Warranty Act.

The next section of this agreement is a disclaimer of consequential damages. As we all remember from first year contract law, the damages under a contract can include consequential damages—under the *Hadley v. Baxendale* rule. The highest potential damages are lost profits. This provision disclaims all such damages for the licensor. Thus, this section is a departure from default law.

The next section of the agreement is entitled "U.S. Government Restricted Rights." This type of language appears in shrink-wrap agreements because the licensor is not aware of the identity of the licensee at the time the agreement is entered into. Certain government regulations, the Defense Federal Acquisition Regulations and the Federal Acquisition Regulations, once provided that any license of intellectual property entered into by a government agency must contain terms for the government to own the intellectual property rights related to the software being licensed. While such a rule worked for custom developments, it was inconsistent with business practice for the off-the-shelf software that began appearing in the marketplace in the 1980s. So, the regulations were modified to allow for a restricted user license in the case of commercial computer software. This section of the agreement identifies the software under this agreement as commercial computer software, so that the explicit terms of the agreement, and not the terms of the federal acquisition regulations, apply to use by a licensee that consists of a U.S. government entity.

The next section of the agreement is entitled "Export Restrictions." This provision binds the licensee to the U.S. export laws. While the licensee, presumably a U.S. entity or person, would be bound by United States export laws regardless of any a provision in an agreement, this provision may assist the licensor to prove that it has used a certain level of efforts to comply, and to force its licensees to comply, with the export laws. The export laws prevent goods from being exported to countries that are under an embargo from the United States or on the list of table of deny orders. Generally, those countries include countries in which the United States is currently involved in political disputes, which currently include, for instance, Cuba, and North Korea. The countries on this list change from time to time, so it is not a good idea to codify them in your contract language.

Finally, the last provision of the agreement contains some general terms. One of these terms is venue selection and governing law selection. Courts do tend to enforce the selection of venue and governing law in agreements, so this can be an important provision. The remainder of the provisions, the integration clause, severability clause, etc., are not terribly different from default law.

Remind Me, Why License?

As you can see, we have identified some, but not many, differences between the law memorialized in this contact and the default intellectual property, contract, and other law that would govern the sale of a copy of a piece of software. So we must return to our original question: Why do lawyers advise the use of license agreements for software, and not for books?

The answer lies to some extent in the differences we identified: limitations on reverse engineering, limitations of liability, limited warranties, dispute resolution and venue. But why do these issues motivate a license agreement for the software but not the book? Reverse engineering does not apply to books, of course. But the UCC governs the sale of books as well as software, and disputes could arise with respect to the sale of any goods.

The answer is that the issues are the same, but the business realities are different. Here are some examples.

Ease of Copying. A book is cumbersome to copy and the copies will be of lower quality than the original. Digital works such as software can easily be copied without degradation of quality. So licensors use license agreements to remind users of the rights of copyright—i.e. that the ownership of a copy does not give a license to copy and distribute the work. Licensors know that they cannot easily police the user's adherence to the terms of the agreement, particularly for minor violations. Thus, the license is not only a legal agreement but a tool of moral suasion—to remind and convince users not to violate the law.

Cost Effective Implementation. A piece of software can force the user to click "I Accept" to use the software, thus reducing the costs of implementing the license in such a way that assent is manifested by the user in an enforceable way. To do so in a book would require a physical implementation like the breaking of seals or shrink wrap, which might increase publishing costs.

Liability. It's difficult to imagine how the content of a book could lead to liability. (In fact, most content-based torts are prohibited by the First Amendment.) But plenty of liability—particularly loss of data and other consequential damages—can arise from the use of faulty software. So licensors use the license agreement to manage this risk.

Disclaimer of Warranties. As discussed above, it is unclear what it means for software to be merchantable. So licensors use the license agreement to avoid liability for bugs.

Jurisdiction and Venue. Greater exposure for liability means greater exposure to lawsuits, so licensors use the license agreement to establish exclusive jurisdiction in their home arena, thus reducing their costs of resolving disputes.

Put all this together, and the answer is that we write licenses when the business context and the potential exposure of our clients, as compared with the transaction costs of implementing the license, makes writing the license worthwhile. This is a good guiding principle for a licensing practice. It is one thing to spot issues and draft language to address all the legal issues that apply to a business situation. But it is quite another to give practical, useful advice to clients that they can implement without compromising their business. To make sure you always do the latter, not the former, always ask: Why? Your client will appreciate your practical approach, and you will avoid the trap of focusing on legal issues so hard that you become blind to your client's business needs.

NOTES

III. Week 2: Contract Basics and Drafting Style

The practice of licensing mainly consists of drafting contracts, reviewing contracts, and negotiating contracts. The tools of this practice are the words of the contracts, and this chapter helps you understand how to use the special tools that compose the type of contracts you will encounter in this practice. First, take a brief look at the contracts in the Forms Appendix to this book. Don't be concerned if the language of the contracts seems difficult to understand. You are learning a new vocabulary, as you would need for any new skill. Once you have looked through the forms, read this chapter, and then when you are done, look at the forms again. At that point, you should feel more comfortable with the type of language in contracts, so you can begin creating them yourself.

Basics of Contract Drafting

The objective of contract drafting is to memorialize the intent of the contracting parties at the time the contract is entered into.(Cal. Civ. Code §1636.) To determine the intentions of the parties, a court will look to the following:

- **Four Corners Rule**. A court first looks to the language of the contract.(Cal. Civ. Code §§1638, 1639.) If the language of the contract is clear and unambiguous, the court will not inquire beyond the contract's language.
- **Evidence Rule** A court will not enforce oral agreements when a written agreement is entered into on the same subject. (Cal. Civ. Code §1641.)

These rules, combined, mean that the written contract is everything. Any rule that you wish to enforce in the relationship needs to be in your contract. With this in mind, here are the basic rules of contract interpretation, which tell you how a court—a judge and jury who were not involved in the drafting process—would view the language there. The quest is for objective meaning, based on the language of the contract, taken at face value.

- **Meaning as a Whole** A writing is interpreted as a whole, and all writings that are part of the same transaction are interpreted together. (Restatements (2d) of Contracts, § 228.)
- **General Meaning**. Where language has a generally prevailing meaning, it is interpreted in accordance with that meaning. (Restatements (2d) of Contracts, § 228.)

- **Technical Meaning**. Technical terms are interpreted according to their technical meaning when used in a transaction within their field. (Restatements (2d) of Contracts, § 228.)
- **Course of Dealing**. Language is interpreted consistent with any relevant course of performance, course of dealing, or usage of trade. (Restatements (2d) of Contracts, § 228.)
- **Effect to All Parts**. Contracts are interpreted first in a way to give a reasonable, lawful, and effective meaning to all the terms, rather than an interpretation that leaves a part unreasonable, unlawful, or of no effect. (Restatements (2d) of Contracts, § 229.)
- **Specific Language**. Specific terms are given greater weight than general language. (Restatements (2d) of Contracts, § 229.)
- **Negotiated Terms**. Separately negotiated or added terms are given greater weight than standardized terms or other terms not separately negotiated. (Restatements (2d) of Contracts, § 229.)
- **Interlineation**. The handwritten portions of a contract will trump the printed portions. (Cal. Civ. Code §1651.)
- **Interpretation against Drafter** Any uncertainties in the language of a contract will be interpreted against the author of the contract. (Cal. Civ. Code §1654.) *If a contract is entered into on April 1, the term of the agreement is specified as being "one full year," and the Licensee (who benefits from a longer term) has drafted the agreement, a court is unlikely to agree with the Licensee's argument that the agreement's term commences on April 1 and continues until 12 months after the following January, or one full calendar year. Instead, the court is likely to favor the Licensor's interpretation that the agreement commences on April 1 and ends the next year on March 31.*
- **Interpretation According to Contract's Purpose**. Any clause that is repugnant to the basic nature of the contract is interpreted in view and subordinate to the contract's purpose. (Cal. Civ. Code § 1652.) *In a non-disclosure provision allowing the use of disclosed information in connection with a technology development, the following provision often appears: "Nothing in this agreement will be construed to restrict either party from developing similar products. However, the foregoing will not be deemed a license to either party's intellectual property rights." If a party argues that the last sentence prohibits use of confidential information because that would require a license of trade secret rights, the court is likely to disagree.*

As you know now after looking at the contracts in the Forms Appendix, the language used in contracts is not the same as the language used in conversation, or even in legal memoranda. Many special words help lawyers to write contracts precisely. This chapter introduces some basic ideas about how to develop your own contract drafting style. Of course, style is a subjective thing, and many lawyers differ a great deal on their thoughts about drafting style. You should consider the following as suggestions, not as mandates. Remember that when you work for supervising attorneys, you will have to adapt to their style. Even if you disagree with another lawyer's style ideas, adapting is a good exercise to help you continue to think critically about your own style habits.

Verbs and Other Language in Contract Drafting

When most people read contracts for the first time, they notice a word that, while almost nonexistent in modern speech, is ubiquitous in contract drafting: "shall." When drafting an agreement, most lawyers rely on the word "shall" without ever knowing why, wondering why, or questioning why they use it. Those who do question seldom find an answer. This is probably because most lawyering skills are learned *ad hoc*, on the job, rather than in a formal training environment. So most lawyers never learn to apply a set of prescribed rules to their contract drafting, but merely imitate the lawyers who have gone before them. This might work, if the same hoary legalisms had not been transmitted from lawyer to lawyer, generation to generation, since the 18th century.

This section discusses different ways to approach using the word "shall" as well as other verbs in contracts, and also discusses general principles on the use of language in contract drafting. The recommendations in this section are based on the principle that contracts written in English should be as close to conventional written English as possible, and that the only reason to use "lawyerly" language is precision. This, in turn, is based on the theory that clients, not just lawyers, should understand contracts. Clients will tell you—at every possible opportunity—that they do not understand "legalese."

Verbs

"Shall" is a conditional or imperative tense of the verb "to be." Most dictionaries describe the correct use of this word in modern speech differently for the first person, as opposed to the second or third person. When speaking or writing formally, one might say, "I shall go to the store," to indicate a statement of present intention (i.e. "shall" is a conditional tense). However, if one says, "You shall go to the store," the sentence is a command (i.e. "shall" is an imperative tense). In contracts, lawyers use "shall" in the second way, as a command.

To understand why lawyers do this, it is important to understand what lawyers mean to accomplish in a contract. A contract is a set of statements of legal obligation. For example, Audrey and Bruce may write and sign a contract that says, "Audrey and Bruce hereby agree that Audrey shall pay Bruce $100 on January 1, 2001." A contract is, in essence, no more than this; the parties state that they have agreed upon certain obligations. When the sentence quoted above is in a legally binding document, "shall" is obviously an imperative. Audrey is legally bound to pay the $100. Of course, it is just as effective to write: "Audrey and Bruce hereby agree that Audrey *will* pay Bruce $100 on January 1, 2001." There is no other reasonable interpretation but that Audrey is legally bound to make that payment. However, what about the following: "Audrey and Bruce hereby agree that Audrey shall pay Bruce $100 on January 1, 2001 and Bruce will put the money in his bank." Is Bruce obligated to put the money in his bank? If so, why did Bruce and Audrey use the word "will" instead of "shall"?

The moral of the Audrey and Bruce story is not that "shall" is better than "will." It is that if you are going to use "shall," use it consistently. If you want to use it in a grammatically and legally correct fashion, that is a noble goal, too—one I share with you—and you will learn how to do that below. But if you do not care to learn to do that, at least use your verbs consistently, meaning you could do any one of the following:

- Use "shall" always
- Not use "shall" at all
- Use "shall" only to create a legal obligation to bind a party to the contract (the correct way)

The "all shall, all the time" option does not require much discussion. Most lawyers already do this, albeit imperfectly. Thus, the following actual excerpt from a contract is quite common:

In the event that Licensor shall have offered to any third party the Products at a price lower than the price Licensor shall be obligated to offer hereunder, Licensee shall have the right to receive the Products at such lower price.

This approach might be ugly, but at least it is consistent. Some lawyers go overboard and make up their own tenses ("until Licensor shall have had to opportunity to review..."), which is amusing, but ultimately harmless. But this approach also leads to the following excerpt, which undoubtedly resulted from an "all shall, all the time" contract being revised by a "shall-less":

> In the event that Licensor shall have offered to any third party the Products at a price lower than the price Licensor shall be obligated to offer hereunder, Licensor will offer the Products at such lower price, upon terms and conditions substantially similar to those offered to such third party.

This result both cries out for misinterpretation and sounds awkward.

The second, "shall-less" approach assumes that lawyers cannot be trusted to use the word at all. Thus, the excerpt above would read:

In the event that Licensor offers to any third party the Products at a price lower than the price of the Products hereunder, Licensor will offer the Products at such lower price, upon terms and conditions substantially similar to those offered to such third party.

This, too, is fine. No sensible person would doubt that, in this contract, the word "will" creates a legal obligation. No clever plaintiff's attorney will be claiming that the "wills" mean less, or something other than, the "shalls."

Finally, the correct, though sometimes confusing, approach uses the following system:

Verb	What it means	Example and *notes*
shall	has a legal obligation to	Licensee shall use its best efforts to distribute the Products. *Only use this verb when the subject is one of the parties to the agreement*
shall not	has a legal obligation not to	Licensee shall not disclose the Confidential Information to third parties.
will	a future occurrence	The Agreement will be governed by California law. *When the subject is not one of the parties to the agreement, you should probably be using this verb instead of "shall."*
must	is required to	All notices must be sent to the address set forth below. *When the subject is not one of the parties to the agreement, but you are emphasizing a requirement, use this instead of "will."*
must not	is required not to	Notice must not be given more than 10 days before the Closing.
may	has the option to	Licensee may terminate this Agreement, for any reason or no reason, upon 10 days' prior written notice. *Permissive.*

After reading the table above, people generally have one of two reactions. Some people find this system bewildering or unnecessary. If you are one of these, you should immediately change to options 1 ("all shall") or option 2 ("shall-less"). The others think, "Now the scales have fallen from my eyes and I see the light!" If you are one of these, the following exercises will help you learn to use this system.

Provision as drafted	Edited Provision	Comments
Definitions. As used in this Agreement, the following terms shall have the meanings ascribed to those terms as hereinafter set forth:	**Definitions**. As used in this Agreement, the following terms have the following meanings:	Simplify verbs and avoid legalism "hereinafter"
Permitted Disclosures. Receiving Party may disclose Confidential Information of Disclosing Party to a court of competent jurisdiction in connection with a subpoena or court order; *provided, however, that Receiving Party shall have given Disclosing Party notice* and opportunity to seek confidential treatment of such Confidential Information.	**Permitted Disclosures**. Receiving Party may disclose Confidential Information of Disclosing Party to a court of competent jurisdiction in connection with a subpoena or court order, *but only if Receiving Party gives Disclosing Party prior notice* and opportunity to seek confidential treatment of such Confidential Information.	"But only if" is simpler than "provided, however, that" and clarifies that the proviso is a condition.
Payments. Licensee shall pay Licensor a royalty of 10% of Net Sales. Each such amount shall be paid no later than 10 business days after the end of the applicable quarter.	**Payments**. No later than 10 business days after the end of each quarter, Licensee shall pay Licensor a royalty of 10% of Net for such quarter.	Avoid passive voice to clarify that the timeliness of the payment is a covenant of Licensee.

Other Language in Contract Drafting

If you want to make your contracts simple and easy to read, here are some suggestions for dispensing with legalisms— language that is never used anywhere but contracts:

Legalism	Correction	Example/Comments
pursuant to	under	
hereunder	under this Agreement	Keep in mind that "hereunder" can also mean "under this Section 1.3," and if so, that is what you should write. Avoiding "hereunder" makes your drafting more precise.
Article 7, Section 7.1(a) above	Section 7.1	Keep section references as short and consistent as possible because they tend to cause typographical errors. If "above" and "below" are redundant, leave them out; if they are not, you need to re-number your contract.
Within 10 days of January 1, 2005.	No later than 10 days after January 1, 2005.	"Within" can mean "before."
The term of this Agreement will be three years after the Effective Date.	The term of this Agreement will commence on the Effective Date and expire 36 months thereafter.	Years can be calendar years. The corrected example is also more precise.
Notwithstanding anything to the contrary herein...	N/A	If what you are writing is inconsistent with some other portion of the agreement, say so explicitly. If you don't know, you have not thought it out well enough.
One Hundred Dollars ($100.00) One Million Dollars ($1,000,000.00)	$100 $1 million	Writing out numbers was originally meant to discourage fraudulent alteration of the contract, which in this

Legalism	Correction	Example/Comments
		age of word processing, faxing, and photocopying is no longer relevant. The "word and number" system causes typographical errors because people tend to change one and not the other, and when they differ, the written words control over the numbers, though they are harder to proofread correctly.
The parties hereto agree that Audrey shall...	Audrey shall...	"The parties agree as follows" is usually at the front of the contract; no need to repeat it.
The parties acknowledge and agree that...	The parties acknowledge that...	
Net Sales, multiplied by a fraction whose numerator is the number of months in such period, and whose denominator is equal to 12.	Net Sales x (number of months in the period)/12	Your client will not understand the first one. Chances are, neither will anyone who is charged with administering the contract.

Sometimes legal language increases precision. The best example is the eradication of the "passive voice." This is a rule of correct writing in general, not just a rule of correct legal writing. In contract drafting, passive voice is especially dangerous, because it does not make clear who bears the obligation. For instance, look at the following actual example:

Each Purchase Order shall be accepted by Seller.

Does this mean the Seller is obligated to accept each purchase order? (This is hard on the Seller, as the Seller may not have the capacity to manufacture all the ordered items.) Does is mean that every purchase order must be accepted by the Seller to be effective? (This is hard on the buyer, because every purchase order can be rejected.)

Here is the correct way to draft it:

Each Purchase Order is subject to acceptance by Seller.
-OR-
Supplier shall accept each Purchase Order.

Here are some more examples of "legal language" that actually works to increase precision:

Language	Correction	Example/Comments
including...	including without limitation...	Unless otherwise defined in a contract, "including" means that the examples following it will be construed as exclusive—instead of its everyday meaning of "for example."
Licensee shall have the right to...	Licensor hereby grants Licensee the right to...	The first can be interpreted as a warranty of non-infringement, the second is a grant of rights.

Just to beat all the points to death, here are a list of ten "commandments" of contract drafting:

1. You shall use verbs consistently.
2. You shall number every paragraph of every contract.
3. You shall place a title or caption on every paragraph of every contract.
4. You shall avoid using the passive voice.
5. You shall define each capitalized term in every contract.
6. You shall not use any word in a contract whose meaning you do not understand.
7. You shall always refer to a corporation as "it" rather than "they."
8. You shall not write long clauses whose only effect is to obscure the obvious.
9. You shall not use legalisms when ordinary language is equally precise.
10. You shall not take drafting rules so seriously that you cease to serve your client.

Parts of a Contract

Now, take a look again at the examples in the Forms Appendix. You should now understand a bit better why the style of writing in these contracts looks the way it does. Also, note how the contract is organized. It usually has these parts:

- **Title**. Titles are subjective and clients tend to have strong preferences about what to call agreements. Avoid using misleading titles, but subject to this rule you should follow your client's wishes. Re-titling an agreement after the client has discussed it with a potential business associate can be confusing. However, avoid using the title "Partnership Agreement" unless you are actually drafting an agreement about operating a partnership entity.

- **Preamble**. This section usually states the effective date of the agreement (which I recommend, rather than dating the agreement on signature lines), the party names and their places of business. Avoid putting obligations or covenants in the preamble.

- **Recitals**. These are the "WHEREAS" clauses. Technically, they are not part of the terms of the agreement, but they can be used to interpret the terms of the agreement.

- **Definitions** (usually section 1). This sections defined the "terms of art" in an agreement, terms that are capitalized against standard usage.

- **Terms and Conditions**. Several (or many) sections and subsections of terms and conditions are in most contracts. Note how they are numbered. Each paragraph should be numbered, so when you are negotiating the agreement, you can specify what portion you are discussing. Use a numbering scheme that is clear and does not necessitate turning pages to determine the unique section of each paragraph.

• **Signature Block**. This lists the parties, who is signing for them, the titles of the signatories, and contains a "By" line on which to sign.

• **Exhibits or Attachments**. These usually contain factual details about the terms and conditions, such as product names, technology descriptions, prices, and ancillary documents. Lawyers use attachment to make an agreement form "modular" or useful for multiple deals, and also to segregate information that should be treated as confidential so the document can easily be redacted.

NOTES

IV: Week 3: The Universe of Deals

You will often hear corporate lawyers say that law school did not prepare them for practicing law. To a law student, this must be inexplicable; after all, law school teaches you about the law and about the process of legal thought. A bright, industrious law student, freshly graduated, could look at a contract and criticize its language; in other words, could spot issues in what is there. But the brightest student cannot tell you what is *not* there. That only comes with experience. Even worse, the student cannot tell you whether it is the right type of agreement for the deal.

A big hurdle in learning how to draft licenses is deciding where to start. What type of deal is this, that a client has described to me? This is a difficult question, because there are so many types of deals. But one objective of drafting a document is to generate a manageable number of comments from opposing counsel, and the best way to do this is to make your drafts look like they contain customary terms for the type of deal. To do this, you need to understand generally the types of deals you are drafting, and familiarize yourself with typical examples of those types of contracts. Then you will develop a sense of what will engender comments and hard negotiation, and what will likely pass unnoticed.

The table below contains some types of technology deals and their characteristics. You should use this list with two caveats. First, every deal is slightly different, and may contain elements of several of the types in the table. This is why transactional lawyers are so useful; few deals lend themselves completely to a pre-written form. Second, clients, and lawyers as well, do not describe these types consistently. So, one lawyer's "OEM deal" may be another lawyer's "publisher license." Your job is not to police the use of these terms, but to develop a consistent understanding of the types of deals in this practice.

Instructor's note: In class, we will find examples in the news stories of the business and technology press and discuss what types of deals they represent.

Product Agreements

Agreement	Description and Comments
Purchase Orders/Invoices	Govern purchase terms for one-time purchases. *Example: Auto parts manufacturer purchases 100 GPS navigation devices*
Supply/Manufacturing	Ongoing sale of goods. One party may manufacture custom goods for another. *Example: Supply Agreement—Disk drive company purchases magnetic media for disks* *Example: Manufacturing Agreement—Fabless semiconductor company hires manufacturer to make its chips*
Sales Agent/Sales Representative	Solicits sales for supplier; supplier enters into sales/license contract directly with

Agreement	Description and Comments
	customer; representative receives a commission. *Example: Software company allows computer hardware company to market its products.*
Reseller or Distributor	Buys products from manufacturer and resells them. *Example: Software company sells its products through a retail outlet.*
Value Added Reseller (VAR)	Buys or makes copies of intellectual property products and sells them bundled with VAR's products. *Example: Software company allows systems integrator to resell its product along with hardware systems that run it.*
OEM	Buys or makes copies of products and sells them under OEM's brand. *Example: Software company with MP3 decoding software allows manufacturer of MP3 player to incorporate the software in the MP3 player.*
Publisher	Makes copies of intellectual property products (such as books or software) and pays developer a royalty. *Example: PC game developer hires a distributor who makes copies of the game and sells them in a foreign country.*
Manufacturing License	License to make goods and sell them to others; pay royalties to licensor. *Example: Optical switch company grants a French company rights to manufacture and sell switches to companies in France.*
Co-Marketing	Neither party sells the other's goods, but they cooperate in sales and marketing activities. *Example: Sales force management software company and e-mail marketing company collaborate to sell their products at a trade show.*

License Agreements

Agreement	Description and Comments
Non-Disclosure	Non-disclosure and non-use of confidential information. *Example: Two companies discuss a potential license agreement and exchange product specifications.*
Test (Beta or Demonstration)	License to test technology; limited rights; no warranties. *Example: Video editing software company gives a free license for a pre-release version of its product to a film studio.*
End User License	License to use technology; minimal copying. *Example: Software company licenses database software to a company for its back-office operations. Includes e.g. Enterprise licenses, Site licenses, Concurrent User licenses.*
ASP	Application Service Provider gives its customers access to software but does not distribute copies. A type of end user license or service agreement. *Example: Payroll check writing service allows customers to enter hours for employees on-line, generate checks.*
Patent License	License to practice a patent. *Example: Owner of a patent covering a method of file compression licenses a company to use that method in its software product.*
Content License	Music or book publishing, licenses to modify and use text, graphics, photos. *Example: Web company licenses graphics and text to put on its web site.*
Escrow	Technology is placed in escrow—usually source code or specifications. *Example: Licensor who distributes an object code version of software escrows source code for benefit of its licensee.*

Development and Services Agreements

Agreement	Description and Comments
Invention Assignment	Independent contractor/employee assigns intellectual property in certain technology to

Agreement	Description and Comments
	customer/employer. *Example: Founder of company assigns rights in a technology product in exchange for shares of stock.*
Services/Developer	One party performs services for another, e.g. consulting; may or may not result in any intellectual property. *Example: Web site development agreement.*
Joint Development	Two parties develop technology together. *Example: Disk drive company and back-up software company collaborate to make their products compatible.*
Outsourcing	Can be quite complicated; one party agrees to take over an entire department or function of the other—typically information services or customer support. *Example: Large company hires a company to provide all of its information services operations.*

Web Agreements

Agreement	Description and Comments
Cross-Linking	This is a trademark license and often also a sales representative arrangement. *Example: Auction site provides a link to an appraising company and vice-versa.*
Co-Branding	This is a trademark license, services agreement and usually also a sales representative arrangement. *Example: Comparison shopping service creates a version of its service branded with the trademark of a credit card.*
Insertion Order	Placement of advertisements on a web site.
Affiliate	This is a sales representative agreement where the affiliate drives traffic to a web site and gets a commission on sales, e.g. the Amazon "Affiliates" program.
Domain Name Transfer	Transfers registration of a domain name.
Bandwidth/Hosting	Gives access to Internet. May include placement of servers in hosting company's premises, i.e. a collocation agreement.

Some Other Agreements

Agreement	Description and Comments
Asset Purchase	The purchase of technology assets often includes assignments and licenses of intellectual property. *Example: Software company sells a product line to another company in exchange for money or stock.*
Cross-Licenses	In some industries it is common for companies with large patent portfolios to license their patents to each other. *Example: Telecom companies cross license to each other all their patents related to a field of use.*
Standards License	Technology companies who wish to promote a uniform standard may cross license any patents they own that are necessary to practice the standard to all comers, in exchange for a license back of the licensee's patents.

Software Distribution Agreements[i]

Commercial distribution agreements and come in many different varieties and can be very confusing. They are most complicated to sort out when they cover products that are licensed rather than sold. Therefore, software distribution agreements are a good example of the various types of commercial agreements, and analyzing them is a useful exercise to understand the business issues involved in product distribution.

While most clients know that they need a distribution agreement, many do not know what kind they need, because they are not familiar with the many options for distributing software and the many kinds of agreement under which software distribution takes place. Unfortunately, commercial distribution agreements are called by many names, which are idiosyncratically and inconsistently used. A "distribution agreement" can mean anything from a channel reseller agreement to an OEM publishing agreement—two types of agreements that can be as different as night and day. This section outlines some of the differences between the various kinds of commercial distribution agreements, you consider what type of agreement your client needs.

Who Makes Copies?—Resellers versus Publishers

Distributors of software are either resellers or publishers. Here are some of the differences that can help you distinguish them:

Reseller	Publisher
Buys packaged goods from the supplier and resells them to customers or other resellers	Makes copies of the software and sells them to customers or other resellers.
Orders software copies from supplier and pays for them based on supplier's invoice	Receives a "gold master" from which to create software copies on its own.
Pays the wholesale price and receives the retail price, keeping the difference (the mark-up).	Pays the supplier a royalty based on units or sales price, and keeps the remainder of retail price.
Reseller pays before products are sold, so cash flow is negative, then positive.	Supplier usually pays in arrears based on actual sales, so cash flow is positive, then negative.
Supplier always knows how many copies are sold	Supplier must rely on reports of publisher to know how many copies are sold
Supplier controls packaging and branding	Publisher is responsible for packaging, which usually requires supplier's approval

Publishing is particularly useful for international distribution. Many software suppliers sell packaged goods to resellers in the United States, but use local publishers to reproduce and distribute goods that have been localized for use in other nations. For those deals, the publisher may also have a license to translate and distribute localized documentation.

Why does this matter? At a minimum, the license grants to a reseller and publisher are very different. Financial terms are quite different. Here are some terms you may find in the agreements:

Reseller	Publisher
Appointment as reseller	License to reproduce and distribute software
Ordering terms, lead times, shipping terms	N/A
Payment terms, credit limits	Royalty terms, minimums and advances
	Reporting, audits
	Quality control
	Confidentiality and security

Whose Brand?—Resellers versus OEMs

The above discussion assumes that the product will be distributed under the manufacturer's brand. More complex distribution arrangements may include the re-branding or co-branding of the product. In this case, the distributor is often called an "original equipment manufacturer" or OEM. (The term "OEM" pre-dates the software industry, and is based on arrangements where a manufacturer produced goods such as spare parts that carried the brand of the better-known supplier. It is thought to be a misnomer when applied to software distribution arrangements, but has persisted in common usage.) Here are some of the differences between a reseller and an OEM:

Reseller	OEM
Supplier controls packaging and branding	OEM may repackage or re-brand the software. Some possibilities: • OEM Product carries OEM brand only • OEM Product is "co-branded," or bears both OEM brand and supplier brand • OEM Product carries a credit or "Intel Inside" type of brand
Product is sold as a stand-alone SKU	OEM usually has an obligation to bundle the supplier's product with its own in a single SKU
Product usually sold at full retail	Prices to OEMs are often heavily discounted and may be "loss leaders"
Products are fully functional	OEMs often use evaluation, "lite," or temporary versions, and allow supplier to do sell-through of upgrades
Supplier usually does first tier technical support to end users	OEM often does first tier technical support to end users, while supplier provides second-tier support to OEM technical staff
Source code is almost never supplied to a reseller	OEMs may need source code to integrate the software with their products

OEM arrangements are most useful when the supplier has poor brand recognition, or the supplier's product is not application software and is therefore unlikely to have value when purchased alone. For instance, low-level utilities, hardware drivers and operating systems are often sold under OEM arrangements in which the supplier's software is integrated into the OEM's application program. Also, many OEMs are computer hardware vendors who "pre-load" software onto computers. This allows the user to purchase a compatible suite of software for an attractive price, making the computer equipment more useful and marketable.

Why is the difference important? The biggest difference is pricing. OEM royalties are usually quite low, either because the supplier is trying to build market share—sometimes hoping to sell upgrades directly to end users—or because the market value of the software is limited.

Variations on a Theme—VARs

Somewhere between a reseller and an OEM lies the value added reseller, or "VAR." A VAR is like a reseller, but a VAR agrees to provide the supplier's products only in connection with other products or services that add value. The VAR is like a hybrid of a reseller and an OEM. Here are some of the similarities:

The VAR...	Which looks like...
Allows supplier to control packaging and branding.	A reseller, which buys boxed goods. VARs are usually publishers only for products that require significant integration.
Has an obligation to bundle the supplier's product with its own.	An OEM, which also bears a bundling obligation.
Sells the product at close to full retail price.	A reseller. If a VAR is allowed to bundle goods for the purpose of pricing, a royalty based on selling price can be problematic.
Sells products that are usually fully functional.	A reseller, which sells stand-alone products.
Provides first-tier technical support to end users, while supplier provides second-tier support to VAR technical staff.	An OEM. The VAR is usually in the best position to perform "triage" on problems, which may stem from the other products sold in the VAR package.

In the software field, VARs go by many names, but some of them may be called systems integrators—which buy software products to sell to end users with hard work on other software as part of a "total solution." Other VARs may be called ISOs or authorized dealers. Once again, the term is not used consistently, and a supplier asking for a VAR agreement can be looking for quite a variety of business terms.

Who Takes Title?—Resellers versus Sales Representatives

Sometimes the differences between a distributor and a sales representative are hard to spot. In certain ways, they behave identically, each trying to solicit orders for products in its territory. Here are some differences.

Reseller	Sales Representative
Buys goods from the supplier and resells them	Solicits orders for products, which are fulfilled by supplier
Orders units from supplier and pays for them based on supplier's invoice	The sales representative does not take delivery of the products and does not collect money or pay for the products
Reseller keeps the difference between the wholesale price and the retail price (the mark-up).	Supplier pays the sales representative a commission based on the selling price
Supplier cannot set the prices the reseller offers to customers; this is "resale price maintenance" that may violate the antitrust laws	Supplier may set prices for a sales representative, because the supplier is the contracting party.

All Other Manner of Creature — Distributors versus Nondescript Species

Recently, the Internet and commercial on-line services have added new types of distribution to the myriad existing relationships between software suppliers and distributors. Some software suppliers have begun distributing software by allowing third party distributors to offer software to customers over a Web page or on-line. This hybrid type of distribution has murky legal underpinnings. Therefore, on-line distribution agreements need to be carefully drafted, and there are no "standard forms" at this time. This chart will show some of the characteristics of an on-line distribution agreement that may make it look like one of the species we have seen before:

Arrangement	Which Looks Like...
Supplier delivers a gold master to the distributor, which places a master copy on its server and allows users to download a copy. Distributor collects fees from end users and pays supplier based on sales.	Publisher
Supplier delivers a gold master to the distributor, which integrates the software with its own software product and allows users to download a copy. Distributor collects fees from end users and pays supplier based on sales.	OEM
Supplier puts a copy of the software on its server, and allows distributor to place a hyperlink to the mechanism for downloading the software. Distributor collects fees from end users and pays supplier based on sales.	Reseller
Supplier puts a copy of the software on its server, and allows distributor to place a hyperlink to the mechanism for downloading the software. Supplier collects fees from end users and pays distributor a commission based on sales.	Sales Representative

The license grants in these agreements have to be reviewed carefully. In the publisher and OEM arrangements, the user actually makes the copy, so it is unclear whether the distributor requires a license to copy the software. Also, the financial terms are difficult to predict. Remember that money flow can be obscured by hyperlinks that make it easy to transparently direct payment from the customer to either to the supplier or the distributor.

Flow of Rights, Flow of Goods

No matter what kind of commercial distribution agreement a software supplier enters into, it is more common for the flow of rights in the software to go directly from the supplier to the end user. This confuses many clients, because the flow of rights and the flow of the goods can diverge. The distributor generally does not use the software for its own purposes. Therefore, it is usually not necessary to license the distributor to use the software (except for limited purposes in connection with installation or technical support). A supplier usually grants a distributor the right to reproduce and distribute software. The right to use the software, however, can be, and usually are licensed directly from the supplier to the end user. The alternative—licensing the right to use the software from the supplier to the distributor, and allowing the distributor to sublicense it to the end user—is rare. Such an arrangement causes enforcement problems, because the supplier does not have privity of contract with the end user.

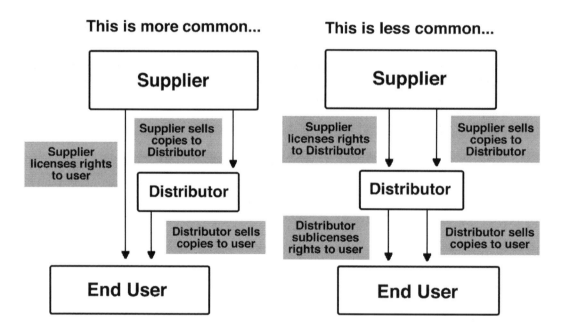

Therefore, most software distribution agreements include a term requiring the reseller or distributor to include the supplier's end user license in the product it distributes to end users. The end user can then enter into the agreement directly with the supplier.

Now that software licenses are changing from shrink-wrap or break-the-seal licenses to "click-wrap" or click-to-accept licenses, these provisions are somewhat less crucial than they used to be. At one time, when shrink-wrap licenses involved packaging the software in a manner such that the user was required to break a seal or shrink-wrap to indicate acceptance of the license terms, it was very important that the supplier had control over the packaging of the software. Failure to include the license agreement or properly print the envelope could void the license. Today, when many licenses are actually embedded in the product, the distributor may only need to promise not to modify the product. However, most software licensing lawyers still recommend a notice on the outside of the package indicating that the purchase of the software copy and use of the software in the package are subject to a license agreement, so packaging approval is still necessary.

NOTES

V: Week 4: Privity and Integration

This section addresses several topics that hang together loosely—which I describe generally under the topics of "Privity" and "Integration."

Privity is a subject that can cause great confusion in legal practice, but there is little formal discussion of it in case law. Privity is defined in *Black's*:

> Privity of Contract: That connection or relationship which exists between two or more contracting parties. (*Black's Law Dictionary*, 6th Edition 1990, p.1199.)

In transactional practice, this translates into a simple question: whose names will appear in the preamble of an agreement? In other words, who is being bound? That this should be a difficult question might seem odd, but most transactional agreements are done between corporations, and many corporations have complex legal entity structures. For a large corporation, the practice of creating subsidiaries and affiliates may be routine and frequent. So it is imperative that you, as attorney, understand whether the corporate entity that constitutes "the other side" of your deal is the correct one.

Often, this is a question of capitalization. If your client is entering into an agreement with a large company, that company will sometimes designate as the contracting entity a wholly-owned subsidiary that has been spun off especially for the purpose of entering into the agreement. However, such an entity is likely not to have significant assets. This can have the effect of making the entity judgment proof. This means, at a minimum, that the indemnity obligations of that entity may be less valuable, because the entity may not have the assets to support the indemnity. This issue can be addressed by requiring the better-capitalized parent guarantee the performance of the subsidiary, or, in some cases, by the maintenance of insurance that would cover the indemnity.

By the way, if you spend the energy and brainpower to resolve this issue, do not let it creep in the back door by allowing the company to freely assign the agreement to affiliates without remaining liable. Contract law tells us that an assignment is generally not considered a novation, but it is probably best to clarify the matter in the assignment clause.

Three Party Agreements

The question of privity is more complex, though, when multiple parties are involved. The most obvious situation is an agreement between three or more parties. If you write a three-party agreement, be sure that all the "boilerplate" provisions still make sense. For instance, in an agreement between ComputerCo, DiskCo, and MovieCo, if DiskCo breaches, who has the right to terminate? Can ComputerCo or MovieCo terminate the agreement as to DiskCo unilaterally, or must they agree? Can either of them terminate the agreement entirely, or only as to DiskCo? There is no easy answer; the best solution will depend on the business context.

Provisions such as dispute resolution also need to be addressed: who can force a dispute to arbitration or litigation? If two parties have a dispute and the third is not involved, what happens?

Also, in a three-party agreement, you will probably need to define the term "third party" before you use it. For instance:

"**Third Party**" means any entity other than a party to this Agreement.

At a minimum, all references to "either party" need to be changed to "any party" for grammatical sense. For instance the following provision:

Notices. Any notice required or permitted under the terms of this Agreement must be in writg and must be: (a) delivered in person; (b) sent by first class registered mail or air mail, as appropriate; or (c) sent by overnight air courier, in each case properly posted and fully prepaid to the appropriate address set forth in the preamble to this Agreement. *Either party may change its address for notice by notice to the other party given in accordance with this Section.* Notices will be considered to have been given at the time of actual delivery in person, three business days after deposit in the mail as set forth above, or one day after delivery to an overnight air courier service.

Should be:

Notices. Any notice required or permitted under the terms of this Agreement must be in writg and must be: (a) delivered in person; (b) sent by first class registered mail or air mail, as appropriate; or (c) sent by overnight air courier, in each case properly posted and fully prepaid to the appropriate address set forth in the preamble to this Agreement. *Any party may change its address for notice by notice to each of the other parties given in accordance with this Section.* Notices will be considered to have been given at the time of actual delivery in person, three business days after deposit in the mail as set forth above, or one day after delivery to an overnight air courier service.

Confidentiality

Confidentiality provisions can be difficult to write for three-party agreements. If two parties are affiliated or otherwise aligned, it may be appropriate to modify the confidentiality provisions accordingly. For instance, take a look at this non-disclosure provision for a transaction in which WebCo Inc. (a U.S. company) enters into an agreement to fund a joint venture in the U.K. (WebCo Ltd.) together with Bricks & Mortar, Ltd., a U.K. company that wishes to leverage its knowledge of bricks and mortar in the Internet space:

Non-Use and Non-Disclosure As used in this Section _____, "**Web Companies**" refers to WebCo Inc. and WebCo. Ltd. together. The Web Companies (on the one hand) and Bricks & Mortar, Ltd. (on the other hand) each agree not to use any Confidential Information of the other for any purpose except to exercise its rights and perform its obligations under this Agreement. The Web Companies and Bricks & Mortar, Ltd. each agree not to disclose any Confidential Information of the other to third parties or to such party's employees, except to those employees of the receiving party with a need to know. Each of the Web Companies and Bricks & Mortar, Ltd. agrees to take reasonable measures to protect the secrecy of and avoid disclosure and unauthorized use of the Confidential Information of the other. Without limiting the foregoing, each of the Web Companies and Bricks & Mortar, Ltd. agrees to take at least those measures that it takes to protect its own most highly confidential information and agrees to ensure that its employees who have access to Confidential Information of the other have signed a non-use and non-disclosure agreement in content similar to the provisions hereof, prior to any disclosure of Confidential Information to such employees.

The agreement between these three entities is a three-party agreement, but because the confidential information of WebCo Inc. and WebCo Ltd. will overlap, and because WebCo Inc. will be operating WebCo Ltd., the "invisible wall" between the confidential information is drawn only between WebCo Inc. and WebCo Ltd., on the one hand, and Bricks & Mortar UK, on the other. WebCo Inc. and WebCo Ltd. can freely use each other's information.

When is a corporation not a corporation? Divisions and Departments.

If you read enough agreements, you will eventually come across a contract that starts like this:

This Manufacturing Services Agreement ("Agreement") is made as of _____, 2001 ("Effective Date") by and between YourClient, Inc., a California corporation with offices at 123 Gizmo Drive, Mountain View, California 94043 ("YourClient") and *the Product Division of UltraMegaCorp, Inc.* a Delaware corporation, with offices at 789 Media Mogul Avenue, Los Angeles, California 90266 ("UltraMega").

The problem is that the "Product Division" is not a legal entity. The accurate way to express this is:

This Manufacturing Services Agreement ("Agreement") is made as of _____, 2001 ("Effective Date") by and between YourClient, Inc., a California corporation with offices at 123 Gizmo Drive, Mountain View, California 94043 ("YourClient") and UltraMegaCorp, Inc., a Delaware Corporation, a Delaware corporation, with offices at 789 Media Mogul Avenue, Los Angeles, California 90266 ("UltraMega"), *by and through its Product Division.*

Non-Competition Covenants

Entity issues come into the spotlight when you write non-competition covenants. Because it is so easy to create subsidiaries, non-competition covenants are often written to capture the entire corporate affiliate structure. For instance, consider an agreement in which B2B agrees to make the products of WaterCo available over its web site. However, B2B is not being paid for developing the portion of its site that will carry WaterCo's offerings; instead, B2B is getting a percentage of revenue from sales of WaterCo's products. This is an attractive arrangement, because in it both parties have an incentive to maximize sales of WaterCo's products. (WaterCo's incentive is implicit; it wants to sell its own products. B2B's incentives derives form the commission structure: the more WaterCo sells, the more commissions B2B gets.). However, this incentive structure will break down if WaterCo sells its products through competing web sites. Therefore, B2B proposes this exclusivity provision:

> **Exclusivity of Efforts**. WaterCo shall not enter into an arrangement with any third party to offer water products and services on-line. For the avoidance of doubt, "on-line" will be deemed to include any wireless, commercial, or other Internet access service including direct web access, or on-line services, such as AOL or MSN.

However, WaterCo may be able to create a subsidiary to enter into the prohibited arrangements, and transfer its products to the subsidiary easily. Thus, B2B should insist on the following:

> **Exclusivity of Efforts**. WaterCo shall not, either directly or indirectly for itself or through its affiliates, enter into an arrangement with any third party to offer water products and services on-line. For the avoidance of doubt, "on-line" will be deemed to include any wireless, commercial, or other Internet access service including direct web access, or on-line services, such as AOL or MSN.

Presumably, WaterCo could circumvent this provision by arranging to sell through a non-affiliated entity, but then its proceeds from the sales are likely to be so diluted that the incentive structure of the WaterCo/B2B agreement will not be compromised. However, WaterCo has a problem. Suppose it is acquired by SuperWorldWaterCo, a global multinational holding company that owns corporations like WaterCo all over the world. SuperWorldWaterCo would then become an "affiliate" subject to this exclusivity obligation. SuperWorldWaterCo may have other on-line arrangements for the products of its other water companies, and violate this provision. At the least, this provision makes WaterCo less attractive as an acquisition candidate, and therefore may actually operate to kill a merger or devalue the shares of WaterCo.

There is no simple answer to this issue. However, one approach is to allow WaterCo to terminate its exclusivity obligations upon an acquisition. B2B will probably insist on some parallel changes to the structure of the deal when such an option is exercised. For instance, any exclusivity obligations of B2B may terminate, B2B may get a right of first refusal to offer any products of the acquiror that are not already available on the Web, or B2B may get the right to terminate the entire agreement or receive compensation for its costs in developing the applicable portions of its site.

Third Parties and Purchase Agreements

Privity issues come up often within the context of volume purchase agreements. For instance, suppose your client, SwitchCo, wishes to enter into a volume purchase arrangement with a large customer, MegaServer. MegaServer may conduct its manufacturing operations through affiliates (if, for instance, MegaServer manufactures several lines of products through different subsidiaries) or third-party contract manufacturers. Therefore, MegaServer wishes all of its affiliates and contract manufacturers to be able to purchase products on the same terms and prices extended to it. This will lead to the type of provisions that follow:

> Subject to the terms and conditions of this Agreement, Supplier agrees to sell Products to Purchaser and Purchaser's Designated Parties under the terms and conditions of this Agreement. For purposes of this Agreement, "Designated Parties" for a Product means each company including, without limitation, Purchaser's manufacturing subcontractors and trading partners, that Purchaser notifies Supplier in writing is authorized to purchase that Product from Supplier pursuant to the terms and conditions of this Agreement. Purchaser will be entitled to withdraw each such authorization by written notice to Supplier, and upon such notice the applicable company shall no longer be a "Designated Party" for that Product. For purposes of volume pricing or other terms or conditions dependent on volume, all purchases of Products by Purchaser and Designated Parties will be aggregated for the benefit of Purchaser and each Designated Party.

The issue for the Supplier here will be that this requires it to do business with all and sundry Designated Parties. It is likely that the Supplier is a larger, better capitalized company than its Designated Parties, who may be small contract manufacturers. Suppliers will often insist that the Purchaser either allow the Supplier the opportunity to accept or reject each Designated Party (by, for instance, running credit checks or making similar inquiries) or that the Purchaser guarantee their performance.

Flow-Down Provisions

One of the most frequent examples of privity issues in the licensing practice is the inclusion of "flow-down" terms in distribution agreements. When a manufacturer sells products directly to a customer, the manufacturer has contractual privity with the customer, by virtue of the purchase order, sales contract, or license agreement that states the terms of the sale. In contrast, when a manufacturer sells products through an intermediary such as a distributor, reseller, VAR, or manufacturing licensee, there is no contractual privity between the customer and the manufacturer. Instead, the contract runs between the customer and the distributor.

However, as you may remember from first year torts, warranty claims, particularly from consumers, do not generally require contractual privity. (The leading case on this point was *Henningsen v. Bloomfield Motors, Inc.*, 161 A.2d 69 (1960). Today the requirement of privity has generally been abandoned in breach of implied warranty actions for consumer goods. See *Prosser and Keaton on Torts*, 5th ed., 1984 § 97, p. 690 et seq.) Thus, a customer can sue a manufacturer for breach of warranty, despite having no direct contractual relationship with the manufacturer. Therefore, manufacturers attempt to limit their exposure by requiring their distributors to enter into contracts with their customers that contain certain provisions limiting the manufacturer's liability. This is not only a question of liability, though. Manufacturers also use flow-down provisions in their contracts with licensees to ensure that the scope of sublicenses granted by the licensee are consistent with their expectations. Here is a typical set of flow down provisions:

- Licensee shall sublicense the Software solely through a written sublicense agreement containing substantially the terms in this Section ___. Upon Developer's request, the Licensee shall provide Developer with a copy of the Licensee's standard sublicense agreement.

- Restrict use of the Software to object code;

- Prohibit (a) transfer of the Software except for temporary transfer in the event of computer malfunction; (b) transfer, lending, lease and rental of the Software; and (c) title to the Software from passing to the sublicensee or any other party;

- Prohibit the reverse engineering, disassembly or decompilation of the Software and prohibit duplication of the Software except for a single backup or archival copy;

- Disclaim, to the extent permitted by applicable law, Developer's liability for any damages, whether direct, indirect, incidental or consequential, arising from the use of the Software;

- Require the sublicensee, at the termination of the sublicense, to discontinue use and destroy or return to the Licensee all copies of the Software and Documentation;

- Require the sublicensee to comply fully with all relevant export laws and regulations of the United States to assure that neither the Software, nor any direct product thereof, are exported, directly or indirectly, in violation of United States law; and

- Specify Developer as a third party beneficiary of the Sublicense agreement to the extent permitted by applicable law.

When you represent a distributor negotiating with a manufacturer, it may seem easy to agree to strict flow-down provisions. Vis-à-vis the customer, the manufacturer and distributor are on the "same side of the table" across from the customer—in other words, in the agreement between the customer and the distributor, the distributors' and manufacturer's interests dovetail. However, while strict provisions may be easy to include in the distributor's form of customer agreement, they can be cumbersome to negotiate with every customer. This puts the distributor in the awkward position of having to check with the manufacturer before making changes in its customer agreements. For this reason, it is best not to agree to include flow-down provisions word-for-word. This explains the use of "substantially" in the preamble of the above example. Also, some distributors are very sensitive to including terms that explicitly name their suppliers, because those terms tend to contradict the image that distributor is generally trying to present to its customers—that of the "complete solution provider."

A Brief Note on Open Source

Open source software licensing is a large topic, mostly beyond the scope of this text. (For more information, see the Open Source Licensing FAQ at www.heathermeeker.com) However, it is worth noting that much of the controversy over open source licensing arises from a set of flow-down provisions: those of the GNU General Public License. This license agreement, which covered the Linux kernel and other open source software, is available at http://www.fsf.org/licenses/gpl.html. This license contains flow down provisions that are, in a way, the mirror image of the typical flow down provisions in commercial licensing discussed above. The GPL requires its licensees to allow redistribution of software, and requires that any re-distributions be made available in source code format. This is what has earned the GPL the epithet "viral" in corporate parlance: once the obligation to lay open source code attaches to software under the GPL, it cannot be foreclosed in further sublicensing. Here is a rough comparison of the types of flow-down provisions in commercial and open source licensing:

GNU GPL	Typical OEM Agreement
Grants right to modify software	Grants right to modify software
Grants right to distribute in source code format	Grants right to distribute in object code format
Requires licensee to disclaim all warranties and limit liability of licensor	Requires licensee to disclaim all warranties and limit liability of licensor
Allows redistribution only under the terms of the GPL	Allows redistribution only under certain minimum terms, usually a standard end user license that only grants the right to use in object code format.
Makes source code freely available.	Makes source code a trade secret.

These terms are so different that, in effect, they change the paradigm for software licensing completely. But they are also similar in the legal mechanism that makes them work—the contractual obligation to set terms to third party licensees.

Integration

Integration is what is required to make a contract a whole, cohesive document. Some transactions involve more than one agreement, or contain additional documents (such as purchase orders, statements of work or specifications) that provide information essential to define the obligations in the agreement. Of course, it is almost always possible to write one, very long agreement that includes all the obligations of the transaction, but most agreements, at a minimum include certain exhibits or schedules that contain factual information.

This separation is done for a variety of reasons. For instance, the securities laws require some companies to file certain agreements with the SEC or otherwise make them available to investors or to the public. Even so, the company filing the document may usually redact certain information—such as prices—from the publicly available version. This is one reason why information is put in exhibits.

But mostly, transactions include multiple documents for the sake of convenience. For instance, in a development deal, the technical specifications for the product to be developed are usually written primarily by engineering or marketing staff. The staff that is primarily tasked with authoring such a document usually works on it in tandem with the drafting of the agreement, so it is easy to attach the document as an exhibit.

Alternatively, one deal point in a transaction might be for one of the parties to enter into a customary relationship with the other. For instance, suppose a computer manufacturer wishes to invest in a software development company. Part of the deal may be the stock purchase to effectuate the investment, and the other part may be a sales arrangement to allow the developer to purchase test equipment at a discount, for use in developing compatible products. A large equipment manufacturer undoubtedly has a form of agreement under which it sells test equipment, so there is no reason to reinvent the wheel. Instead of writing a custom agreement with both the terms of the stock purchase and the terms of the equipment sale, the parties may enter into the stock purchase agreement, with the form of equipment purchase attached. This is even more efficient where the attorneys handling the different agreements are from different practice areas. Coordinating work on a single document may be logistically difficult, and working on separate documents may be easier.

Finally, sometimes documents are separated for tax purposes, to support an interpretation that the transaction memorialized by each document is an independent transaction with its own tax treatment. It is important to follow the advice of a tax lawyer or adviser when engaging in this practice; however, it is also important to point out any business ramifications (differences in limitations of liability and cross-breach issues, for instance) that will result from separating documents for tax purposes.

If you are working on a deal with multiple parts, just be sure that some document references them all. This will likely be accomplished in the "Integration" section of the agreement—which is usually in the miscellaneous terms at the end of the agreement, or better yet, in the recitals.

NOTES

VI: Week 5: Ownership and Transfer of Intellectual Property

One of the most complex tasks in technology licensing is the drafting of ownership provisions. This task is difficult because ownership provisions are most useful to agree on before the development takes place. But while it may be best to decide on ownership before the development begins, that is the time it is most difficult to allocate ownership of intellectual property, because the underlying technology does not yet exist. Lawyers often end up in negotiation battles over ownership—which can be an emotional issue for clients—with little idea of the prize the battle is meant to win.

Of course, it is not necessary to draft an agreement to allocate the ownership of intellectual property. There is a wealth of background law that controls who owns intellectual property in the absence of an agreement. But it is important to know when to keep the contract silent (i.e. when background law clearly favors your client and for business reasons the issue should not be negotiated) and when to call the issue out. Also, written ownership provisions help corporations keep their intellectual property house in order, to assist them in the due diligence process. (See the discussion in the last chapter of this book on Assignment in Miscellaneous Provisions, for an explanation of the due diligence process and why it is important.)

To carry on a licensing practice, you need to understand the ownership of intellectual property, its operation and implications, extremely well. A couple of concepts may help you.

Things Are Not Ideas.

First, there is a difference between products or information that exist in the real world—like technology, text, pictures, gizmos, and whatever else your client may be marketing or selling—and intellectual property. This is like the difference between a house and the deed to the house. Strictly speaking, the product of a joint development project is not intellectual property, it is technology. You should always draft agreements with this in mind. For instance take the example of Guesstimate and BFGMC in the hypotheticals in the Appendix. The two want to collaborate to develop a software-based messenger routing system, and let us suppose that BFGMC wants to own the resulting rights. This is wrong:

Definition. "Messenger Routing Software" means all software, documentation, copyrights, patents, and trade secrets developed by the parties hereunder.

...

Assignment of Rights. Guesstimate hereby assigns to BFGMC all right, title and interest in and to the Messenger Routing Software.

And this is right:

Definition. "**Messenger Routing Software**" means all software, documentation, works of authorship, invention, and proprietary information or processes developed by the parties hereunder.

...

Assignment of Rights. Guesstimate hereby assigns to BFGMC all right, title and interest in and to the Messenger Routing Software and all copyrights, patent rights, and trade secret rights therein.

This may seem a technical distinction, but it will help you in your drafting. For instance, your agreement will probably have terms requiring one party to deliver a copy of the Messenger Routine Software to the other, or granting Guesstimate a license to use it. If you have defined this term the first way, including intellectual property rights, then your provisions requiring delivery of the software will require the physical delivery of a copyright and patent right, and that is nonsensical.

Enabling Rights

The different kinds of intellectual property protection vary greatly in what they allow their owners to do. All intellectual property rights are limited to the ability to exclude others from practicing them. So, owning a copyright or a patent does not, theoretically, give you the right to do anything—merely the right to prevent others from doing so. However, under copyright and trade secret law, independent invention is a defense to infringement, so owning a copyright or a trade secret effectively gives one the right to use the covered materials without fear of copyright or trade secret infringement. Patents, on the other hand, do not give anyone the right to do anything, because independent invention is not a defense to infringement. Thus, a patent owner may license to a licensee the right to use a patent, but that does not guarantee that any product of licensee claimed in the patent (i.e. that the patent owner could prevent the licensee from making or selling, but for the license) will not violate other persons' patents, copyrights, and the like. Trademarks are mostly like patents; owning a mark in one jurisdiction or market does not guarantee that the use of a mark in another jurisdiction will be non-infringing, because others may have superior rights there. Likewise, ownership of a trademark registration does not guarantee that the use of a mark will be non-infringing, because registration is only evidence of ownership, not ownership itself.

For this reason, copyrights and trade secrets are sometimes called "enabling rights" and patents and trademarks "non-enabling rights." This means that a license to practice a patent or trademark is not usually thought to be a "clearance" of the right. In other words, the licensee is still bearing a risk of infringement despite having the license. (For a more in-depth discussion of this issue, see the chapter on warranties and indemnities.)

The various forms of intellectual property thus are quite different in operation and scope. To fully understand this, you should start by thinking about how ownership arises for each kind of protection. This is the first step in understanding how to effectuate different ownership schemes in your contracts. The next step is to understand how ownership arises in corporations, when corporations themselves are not, strictly speaking, authors (under copyright) or inventors (under patent).

How and When Ownership Arises

Patents	To be patentable, and invention must satisfy the requirements of subject matter, novelty, utility, non-obviousness as described in Title 35 of the U.S. Code. But patent protection (i.e. the ability to sue to enforce the patent) only arises after the inventor has filed a patent application, and patent has been issued on the application.
Copyrights	Copyright ownership arises automatically when a work of authorship with sufficient originality (which has a low threshold) is fixed in a tangible medium. Under the Berne Convention, no formalities (e.g. registration or notice) are necessary for ownership.
Trade Secrets	Trade secret "ownership" vests automatically in the creator of information that satisfies all the requirements for trade secret protection (under the Uniform Trade Secrets Act, i.e. that derives an economic benefit from being kept a secret, and for which reasonable efforts have been made to keep it a secret). There is no registration system.
Trademarks	Trademark "ownership" arises when a trademark is used in commerce. Registration is not required but provides evidence of use and constructive notice.

"Work For Hire": How does a corporation come to own intellectual property?

For patents and copyrights, the inventor or author generates the subject matter of the intellectual property, i.e. the invention and the work of authorship. But corporations also wish to own these rights, and because corporations, strictly speaking, cannot invent or author anything, they use two methods to obtain these rights. For patents, they use assignments and shop rights. For copyrights, they use assignments and the operation of the "work for hire" doctrine.

Patentable inventions are the personal property of the inventor. The individual inventor owns the patent rights in inventions, even if that subject matter was conceived or reduced to practice during the course of employment. However, an employer may have an irrevocable, non-exclusive and nontransferable royalty-free license to use an employee's patented invention (a "shop right") if the invention was conceived or reduced to practice using the employer's resources, facilities, or time. This does not mean that the employee has transferred rights in the invention to the employer, merely that the employer has a non-exclusive license to use it.

An employee may have a duty to assign rights in an patentable invention to his employer under an express contract. Such an assignment must be in writing to be enforceable.(*See* 35 U.S.C. § 261; *also see* Cal. Bus. & Prof. Code § 22372.) This is generally accomplished using an employment assignment agreement, which is signed when the employee hires on.

Under copyright law, the author of the work is the copyright owner. (17 U.S.C. § 201(a).) Authorship of a copyright is determined at the time the work is fixed in a tangible medium. Authorship can never be transferred, though the rights in the resulting copyright can be assigned. However, a corporation can gain the rights directly if a work is designated as a "work for hire," in which case the employer is considered the author for copyright purposes. (17 U.S.C. § 201(b).)

"Work for Hire" is one of the most misused and poorly understood concepts in intellectual property law. Designating intellectual property as work for hire is tempting, but it is also a trap in California. First, it is arguable whether any work can be designated a "work for hire" by contract, because federal law governs what constitutes work for hire, and it is unclear whether a contract governed by state law can change that, due to the preemption of the Copyright Act. (17 U.S.C. § 301.) According to 17 U.S.C. § 101, a "work for hire" is either (a) "work prepared by an employee within the scope of his or her employment" or (b) a work that falls into one of the nine categories specified in the statute[ii] as specially commissioned work, as long as there is an express written agreement that the work is a work made for hire.

Unless a work falls into one of these nine categories, a work is only a "work for hire" if the author is an employee, not an independent contractor. Courts rely on general principles of agency law to determine whether an independent contractor relationship exists, and construe the statute strictly to the benefit of the employee or author, based on a balancing test that examines the facts of the authorship context.[iii]

A strong argument can be made that, other than for works in the nine categories, claiming work for hire status in a contract is of no effect. The effect of a work being a "work for hire" is to remove it from the termination of transfers provisions of the Copyright Act, which allow authors to revoke certain assignments and licenses of copyrights.[iv] A "work for hire" is not subject to the termination provisions that apply to assignments and licenses, because the ownership of such a work vests automatically in the employer. The termination of transfers rules were drafted expressly to protect authors and their heirs, and cannot be contracted away. Thus, it is unlikely that any court would recognize a contractual designation of a work for hire if the work were not one under default law.

But even worse, the arbitrary designation of work product as work for hire can harm a corporation claiming its benefits. In California, there is a rebuttable presumption that a worker performing services to create works for hire is an employee rather than an independent contractor. (Cal. Lab. Code § 2750.5.)

Employers who choose to regard their authors as employees in order to take of advantage of the "work for hire" doctrine in copyright law may also be required to provide employment benefits under California law. (Cal. Lab. Code § 2750.)

Also, employee assignments are limited by a public policy rule in California. Under California law, a provision in an employment agreement requiring assignment of inventions does not apply to inventions developed solely using the employees resources, facilities, or time, except if the invention relates to the employer's business or results from work performed for the employer.(Cal. Lab. Code § 2870.) However, the employee may have a duty to assign rights in an invention to his or her employer if the employee was (a) specifically hired to exercise his or her "inventive faculties," or (b) has a fiduciary relationship, such as an officer or director of a corporation, to his employer.

Joint Authorship: The Road Down the Garden Path

Many clients try to solve the problem of apportioning ownership in intellectual property contracts by proposing "joint ownership." Although joint ownership can work for some types of intellectual property, it is seldom the most desirable approach for either owner. Joint ownership means that either owner can, absent an agreement to the contrary, exercise rights in the jointly owned property. As a corollary, either party can license others to practice those rights. So, if the nature of intellectual property ownership is to be able to prevent others from exercising rights in the intellectual property, joint ownership leaves neither owner in a true ownership position. Neither party can prevent others from taking a license from the other joint owner, and neither party can grant an exclusive license to anyone else.

Moreover, joint ownership creates some unexpected consequences. Under United States copyright law, a joint owner is under a duty to account to the other joint owners of the work for the profits realized from his or her use of the work. (*Oddo v. Ries*, 743 F2d 630 (9th Cir. 1984).) This is not an obligation to pay royalties (i.e. a right of contribution)—it is only an obligation to provide an accounting. Under patent law, the consequences of joint ownership can prove fatal to a patent application. For joint inventors, anything that would constitute prior art in the application for a patent of either of the individual inventors constitutes prior art to the application both inventors jointly. This prior art could prevent a patent from issuing because the invention would then fail its novelty requirement. This is quite counter-intuitive to most clients. Finally, standing and joinder issues can make lawsuits to enforce jointly owned patents problematic.

Who Will Own Intellectual Property?

To draft your agreement correctly, you and your client must determine who will own the intellectual property that results from the development activities to be performed. As noted above, this task can be daunting before either side knows exactly what will be developed. Clients may spend surprisingly little effort thinking about this issue before the deal reaches a definitive agreement, so it can be a point that engenders much negotiation.

In development arrangements where one party is a customer and the other a professional development shop, it is customary for the customer to receive a transfer of intellectual property rights if it is paying full fees for the development. However, if the customer is paying a discounted rate or the development uses materials already developed by the developer, the customer often receives a partial assignment or a license only. Assignments are also more common when the materials being developed will become part of the customer's core product, less common when they are ancillary to the customer's business.

If you come to a roadblock negotiating ownership, the answer is sometimes to allow the developer to keep the rights, in exchange for a contractual agreement not to use the rights in favor of the customer's competitors. If the duration of that negative covenant is equal to the development lead time for the developer's next project, it will be of little real cost to the developer, while addressing the customer's need to have the "first-to-market advantage" with the developed technology.

Another way to break through an impasse in ownership negotiations is to set up a procedure to determine ownership during the performance of the agreement, rather than determining it *ex ante*. Thus, a customer and developer who plan to prepare a statement of work for the technical steps in a development project may also designate in the statement of work who will own the resulting intellectual property. It can be of great advantage to your client to have the "default" in its favor. In other words, if you represent a developer, propose that the developer will retain ownership of everything except what is otherwise designated as owned by the customer in the statement of work.

Other than in development deals, assignments of rights are unusual, except in acquisitions, or in agreements of the founders of a company to assign rights in exchange for equity or other consideration. Most other deals involve licenses instead of assignments of rights.

How to Assign Intellectual Property

Once you have decided who should own the intellectual property arising from a business activity, you need to draft your agreement accordingly. To do this correctly, you need to clarify whether or not a transfer is taking place. Thus, if as in our hypothetical, Guesstimate is doing all of the development and intends to hold on to the rights that will automatically vest in it in the course of the development, the proper drafting is:

Guesstimate will retain all right, title and interest in and to the Messenger Routing Software and all intellectual property rights therein.

In contrast, if BFGMC will own the resulting intellectual property, the following is proper:
Guesstimate hereby assigns and shall assign to BFGMC all right, title and interest in and to the Messenger Routing Software and all intellectual property rights therein.

Note that the language above includes present language of transfer, as well as a covenant to transfer in the future. The following is incorrect and will not clearly effectuate a transfer:
BFGMC will own all right, title and interest in and to the Messenger Routing Software and all intellectual property rights therein.

But what if your client is Guesstimate, and you wish to wordsmith in a way that will favor your client? Here is a suggestion:

"**Work Product**" means all software code, technical and end user documentation, flow charts, specifications, and any other works of authorship delivered to BFGMC hereunder.

…

Guesstimate hereby assigns and shall assign to BFGMC all right, title and interest in and to the Work Product and all intellectual property rights embodied therein.

This language ("works of authorship") arguably does not transfer ideas or inventions—which are trade secrets, and possibly a basis for patent protection. This is important for a developer that wishes to re-use the ideas and methods it develops for its next project. This will be particularly important for developers whose primary line of business is consulting, as they will probably need to re-use their ideas for the next client.

Finally, if you are seeking to transfer intellectual property that is already in existence (as opposed to intellectual property that will arise from performance of the contract) be sure to assign the right to sue based on past infringements, as well.

Quitclaim Grants

If you are working for an assignor of intellectual property rights, you should understand how to write a quitclaim grant, and when it is appropriate. A quitclaim grant is a grant that transfers all of the assignor's interest in property, but does not purport to transfer all rights in the property. For instance, in the following example:

> Assignor hereby grants to Assignee all *of Assignor's* right, title and interest in and to the Software and all *of Assignor's* intellectual property rights therein.

The underlined words make the grant a "quit-claim" grant. This means that others may own an interest in the intellectual property rights, but Assignor does not intend to assign them. In a way, of course, all assignments only operate to transfer the interest of the assignor, because that is all the assignor has the power to grant. But if the underlined language is missing, absent a warranty disclaimer, the grant might be interpreted to imply that Assignor is warranting that it owns all the rights in the materials and rights being transferred.

The Transfer of Trademarks

Particular care is necessary when assigning rights in trademarks. This is a well known malpractice trap: transferring a mark without transferring the attendant goodwill is known as an "assignment in gross," which can dilute rights in the mark, sometimes rendering it impossible to enforce. When you transfer a trademark, always transfer the mark "along with all the goodwill attendant thereto." This issue is easiest to miss in assignments of "all intellectual property" associated with a business relationship. Careful drafting requires that trademarks should either be excepted from the assignment, or transferred along with their goodwill. Note that development projects usually do not give rise to trademark rights—because trademark rights do not arise from invention, but from use in commerce.

NOTES

NOTES

VII: Week 6: License Grants

Writing license grants is the core task in drafting a license agreement, and writing them correctly requires thorough thinking about the deal and what gives it value. At a minimum, you should understand five things about the license to begin writing it: exclusivity, territory, term, royalty, and scope.

Exclusivity

Exclusivity is the most important term of a license agreement. But the word "exclusive" can be ambiguous. For instance, if Licensor grants to Licensee an exclusive right to distribute a product, it is clear that Licensor cannot grant the same right to someone other than Licensee. But can Licensor still distribute the product on its own? Sometimes, a license where the Licensor reserves the right to exercise the license itself is called a "sole" license, as opposed to an "exclusive" license. However, particularly when you are representing a licensee, it is best to be clear. For instance, the following is an exclusive distribution license: Licensor hereby grants to Licensee the exclusive right to distribute the Products. For avoidance of doubt, in the foregoing sentence, "exclusive" means that Licensor shall not for its own account, and shall not grant to any third party the right to, distribute the Products.

The following is a "sole" license:

Licensor hereby grants to Licensee the exclusive right to distribute the Products. For avoidance of doubt, in the foregoing sentence, "exclusive" means that Licensor may distribute the Products, but shall not grant to any third party the right to distribute the Products.

One important implication of the exclusivity terms of a license is standing to enforce the rights being licensed. Under United States law, an exclusive licensee usually has standing to bring a suit to enforce the exclusively licensed rights. A non-exclusive licensee does not. So, for instance, a licensee that has received an exclusive license to a patent may bring a patent infringement suit against a third party infringing the patent, even though the licensee is not the owner of the patent. A non-exclusive licensee has no such standing.

Also, in exclusive licenses, it is customary for the licensor to enter into obligations to enforce the rights against third parties, or to assist the licensee in doing so. This is because, for an exclusive licensee, third party infringement decreases the value of the license, which allows the licensee to practice the intellectual property to the exclusion of all others. For a non-exclusive licensee, third party infringement would have much less effect on the value of the license, because the licensee would expect third parties to be practicing the intellectual property.

As a corollary, some owners of patents categorically refuse to grant exclusive licenses. They do not want to allow the licensee the ability to enforce the patent in their name. This largely arises for what are called defensive patent portfolios. Suppose a disk drive company, DiskZilla, holds a patent on a disk drive. Its competitor, DiskOrama, holds a patent on a disk manufacturing process. In fact, each is infringing the other's patent, but they do not sue each other. Partly, this is because of deterrence, like nuclear powers who never push the button. If one sues, the other counter-sues. Also, it is because insofar as patents are like nuclear weapons, they are like nuclear weapons that have never been tested. A patent infringement lawsuit is usually answered by a counterclaim that the patent is invalid, and sometimes these counterclaims are successful. Once the patent is adjudged invalid, it cannot be enforced against any party. Thus, the patent may be more valuable as a potential weapon than as a real one.

Now, imagine that an exclusive licensee can bring suit to enforce the patent. An enforcement suit can result in invalidation of the patent, which leaves the licensor unprotected. Also, if a licensee of DiskOrama sues DiskZilla, DiskZilla may sue DiskOrama in turn. To complicate matters, many competitors in technology industries enter into patent cross-licenses which can be invalidated if a licensee sues to enforce a patent. For instance, DiskZilla and DiskOrama may enter into an agreement not to sue each other based on their patent portfolios—much like a treaty among well-defended nations. But if one licensee sues, the agreement can be terminated: if one ally drops a bomb, the truce is off.

Thus, some licensors insist on granting licenses that are non-exclusive, but, as a trade-off, agree to a non-competition clause in the field of what otherwise would have been an exclusive license. If you plan to take this route, and whenever you draft non-competition clauses, be careful not to run afoul of the antitrust laws by creating a price fixing or output restriction scheme.[v]

Territory

The next most important parameter for the scope of a license is territory. A grant with limited territory serves the licensor, because the licensor can select different licensees to best serve different territories based on local connections, language and cultural proficiency, or the enforceability of the intellectual property rights in various jurisdictions.

Territorial limitations are most important for what are sometimes called the commercial rights: under copyright, these are distribution, public performance and public display (i.e. not reproduction or preparing derivative works); and under patent, these are sale and import (not manufacture or use). Licensors who divide their licensing programs by territory are usually trying to control where goods are sold, not where they are developed or manufactured. Thus, the following grant may not be optimal:

Licensor hereby grants to Licensee the right to make, have made, use, sell and import the Products in the Territory.

The Licensee may legitimately claim that this is too restrictive, and that the grant should instead read:

> Licensor hereby grants to Licensee the right to make, have made, and use the Products. Licensor also hereby grants to Licensee the right to sell and import the Products in the Territory.

But what exactly does it mean to sell in a territory? Does it mean to sell to customers located in the territory? To customers domiciled in the territory? To anyone at a location in the territory? This question may be difficult enough for traditional physical distribution of goods. For on-line deals, where sales can be made easily accessible worldwide, territories can be even more difficult. If a licensee has a grant to sell products over a web site, can there be any territorial limitations? These questions are important to clarify when you are helping your client determine the business points of a deal. (To make things worse, in the E.U., certain territorial restrictions are unenforceable, as the law in the E.U. favors free trade between the member nations.)

Term and Royalty

The term of a license is one of the most difficult and most overlooked elements of a licensing deal. First, it is important to understand that license agreements have two terms: the term of the agreement and the duration of the license grant. Sometimes these two are the same, sometimes not. But you should always be very clear about both of them. The most ambiguous example is this:

> Section 1. **License**. Licensor hereby grants to Licensee a non-exclusive license to reproduce and distribute the Products.
>
> Section 2. **Term**. The term of this Agreement will be five years.

What happens in five years? Does the license continue beyond the term of the agreement? The best answer is probably that it does not, because, with no suggestion to the contrary, the terms of a written contract are only in effect until its expiration. But the following two examples are better.

Term License Grant

Section 1. **License**. Licensor hereby grants to Licensee a non-exclusive license, during the term of this Agreement, to reproduce and distribute the Products.

Section 2. **Term**. The term of this Agreement will be five years.

Survival Provision

Section 1. **License**. Licensor hereby grants to Licensee a perpetual, non-exclusive license to reproduce and distribute the Products.

Section 2. **Term**. The term of this Agreement will be five years. The grant of license under Section 1 will survive any expiration of this Agreement.

Remember that you must understand the term and scope of a license to understand the pricing for it, and vice-versa. A software end user license that is payable up-front in a lump sum is often perpetual. A license to distribute software products that is payable up-front in a lump sum is usually term-limited. Any license that requires the payment of yearly fees is usually either time-limited to the period to which the fee pertains, or terminable on non-payment.

Finally, particularly when you grant licenses to patents, you should be careful not to grant a license that exceeds the term of protection of the patent. If a licensor grants a license that bears running royalties and survives the term of the valid patent, this can be viewed as patent misuse, and result in antitrust liability or inability to enforce the patent.

Scope and Field of Use

A common restriction on the scope of a license grant is a "field of use." This is similar to a territorial restriction, but instead of a geographic restriction, it is a market segmentation restriction. Thus, if the licensor has developed a product such as a lubricant, the licensor may grant one licensee the right to manufacture and use it in automobile engines, and another the right to use it in rocket motors. Each of these field-restricted licenses can be exclusive or non-exclusive. The way to accomplish a field of use restriction is:

> Subject to the terms and conditions of this Agreement, Licensor hereby grants to License a worldwide, royalty-bearing license under Licensor's interest in the Intellectual Property to make, have made, sell, offer to sell, import and use products in the Field of Use.

Drafting License Grants

Now that you have decided the parameters of the license you wish to draft, you need to learn the words that compose the "formula" of a license grant. First, license grants should always include present language of grant, thus:

Licensor hereby grants to Licensee the right to……

And not:

Licensor shall grant to Licensee the right to……

This is a technicality: courts rarely grant specific performance for contracts, and even when they grant injunctive relief, they usually prefer negative (i.e. an order to refrain from acts) to positive (i.e. an order to engage in acts) injunctions. The first grant in the example is effective as of the date the agreement begins. The second gives Licensor the opportunity to claim that the license has not been granted, but must be granted in the future. If so, and Licensee seeks to enforce the contract, Licensee may only get damages, and not a license.

There are two approaches to writing license grants. The first ("formal") approach is to list the rights enumerated in the applicable statute (e.g. copyright or patent). The second ("functional") approach is to say what the license is able to do in business terms, and not list the rights. Either of these can be appropriate, depending on the situation. Patent licenses almost always use the first approach. Licenses that do not fit well in to the scheme of the statute are often written the other way. The best example is a software end user license, which, as discussed in the first chapter in the context of a shrink wrap license agreement, grants the right to "use" software. Because "use" is not a right under copyright, this represents the second approach. Here is an example of each for a software end user license:

Functional Approach

Licensor hereby grants to Licensee the right to use the Software for its internal business purposes.

Formal Approach

Licensor hereby grants to Licensee the right to reproduce the Software as necessary for Licensee to use the Software for its internal business purposes, and as necessary for Licensee to create a reasonable number of backup copies of the Software.

Note that the latter approach requires more thought, and it is possible to miss the evocation of some rights in collateral activities, such as making backup copies. And yet few would read the first example as preventing backup copies.

The rights that you might license under the various intellectual property schemes are:

Type of Right	Right	Meaning
Patent	Make	To manufacture a product
	Have made	To engage an agent to manufacture a product for sale by licensee
	Use	To use a product
	Sell, offer for sale	To sell a product or place it on sale
	Import	To import a product into the United States
	Practice method	To practice the method in a method patent
Copyright	Reproduce	To make copies
	Distribute	To give to another party
	Prepare derivative works of	To modify
	Publicly perform	To publicly present a sequential work such as a play, movie, or song
	Publicly display	To publicly present a non-sequential work such as a painting or photograph
Trade secrets	Use	To use for any purpose to commercial advantage
	Disclose	To make available to a third party

License grants are written in a kind of code, which includes a laundry list of adjectives. Here are a few of them:

Licensor hereby grants to Licensee a...

Description	Notes
"non-exclusive" or "exclusive"	"Exclusive" is always ambiguous. Is the grant exclusive as to the licensor? Better to draft a provision saying what the licensor will not do, e.g. "grant to any third party the right to..." or "for its own account or for the benefit of any third party, engage in..."
"non-transferable"	May require exceptions if license can be assigned in connection with corporate transactions.
"sublicenseable" or "non-sublicenseable"	Distinguish between sublicensing and "have made" rights.
"worldwide"	As an alternative, you may grants rights in a territory. If you do this, think carefully about what rights need to be exercised only in the territory and which can be worldwide. For instance, a publisher may be able to make copies anywhere, but may be able to distribute in the territory only.
"perpetual" or "during the term of this Agreement"	"perpetual" is ambiguous, but usually means not for a given term. Often the license grant ends with the termination of the agreement, but the license is still described as "perpetual."
"irrevocable"	Usually means the license cannot be terminated, but check the survival provisions of the agreement to see whether the license survives termination.
"royalty-free," "fully paid-up" or "royalty bearing"	Royalties usually mean ongoing payments, so "royalty-free" can be ambiguous. Use "fully paid-up" when there is a one-time up-front payment.
"limited" or "unlimited" "personal" or "for internal purposes"	Not very meaningful; try to draft these limitations more specifically. What can the licensee do? What is the licensee restricted from doing?

"...license to..."

"reproduce" "distribute" "prepare derivative works of" "publicly perform" "publicly display"	Current copyright rights
"transmit" "provide access to"	Neighboring rights under treaties and proposed legislation
"make" "use" "sell" "import"	Patent rights under Title 35 (goods)
"have made" "offer for sale"	Other patent rights
"practice the method"	Patent rights (methods)
"use" "disclose"	Trade secret "rights"

Subject of Grant

Think carefully about the subject of the grant. For copyrights, name the copyrightable materials. For trade secrets, name the information. For patents, describe the goods or methods. You should use terms of art you have defined for the technology. This is where it helps a great deal to have written separate definitions for technology and intellectual property, instead of improperly lumping them together.

Some other restrictions for software licenses:

"solely for its internal use and not for the benefit of any third party, including without limitation "service bureau" use"	"Internal Use" or "Enterprise" license
"solely for use by the number of 10 [simultaneous] users"	User restriction (seat license) [Simultaneous user restriction]
"solely for use at Licensee's premises located at _____"	"Site" license
"solely for use on the following central processing unit _____"	"CPU" license
"solely in the field of"	Field of use restriction
"solely in connection with the simultaneous distribution of _____"	"OEM" or bundling license

Trademark Licenses

Trademark licenses are less common than other types of licenses. This is partly because they are often not necessary. A distributor of a product made by a certain manufacturer may use the trademark of the manufacturer in advertising, in certain customary ways, without an explicit license. In fact, trademark licenses in the context of distribution and sales representative agreements (where they are most common), are usually used to bind the distributor to certain approval and review procedures for use of the mark, rather than strictly to effectuate the license. Thus, a typical trademark license provision in a distribution agreement looks like this:

> **License**. During the term of this Agreement, Licensor grants to Licensee the right to advertise the Software under the trademarks, marks and trade names that Licensor may adopt from time to time ("Marks"), solely in connection with the distribution of Products pursuant to this Agreement.
>
> **Use**. Licensee shall apply, display and reproduce at least one of the Marks, in the size, place, and manner Licensor may indicate from time to time, on each of the Products and related materials, including without limitation cartons, advertisements, sales literature, user documentation, and promotional materials ("Promotional Materials"). Licensee shall use such Marks only in a manner that complies in all material respects with Licensor's policies in effect from time to time.
>
> **Quality Control and Approval of Trademarks**. Licensee shall ensure that Licensee's **[distribution]** services in connection with the Software will be consistent with the historical quality of goods and services used in connection with the Marks. Licensee shall submit to Licensor all representations of the Marks that Licensee intends to use in connection with the Products or any related Promotional Materials, for Licensor's approval of design, color, and other details. Licensee shall not publish, disseminate, exhibit, or otherwise distribute any such material, without Licensor's prior approval.
>
> **Assignment of Goodwill**. If Licensee, in the course of performing its services hereunder, acquires any goodwill or reputation in any of the Marks, all such goodwill or reputation shall automatically vest in Licensor when and as, on an on-going basis, such acquisition of goodwill or reputation occurs, as well as at the expiration or termination of this Agreement, without any separate payment or other consideration of any kind to Licensee, and Licensee agrees to take all such actions necessary to effect such vesting. Licensee shall not contest the validity of any of the Marks or Licensor's exclusive ownership of them. During the term of this Agreement, Licensee shall not adopt, use, or register, whether as a corporate name, trademark, service mark or other indication of origin, any of the Marks, or any word or mark confusingly similar to them in any jurisdiction.

However, trademark licenses do occur outside the distribution context, usually in manufacturing agreements. If you do this type of license for a trademark owner, you must ensure that the goods to which the trademark is applied adhere to a standard of quality at least as high as that used by the manufacturer for its own goods sold under the same mark, or you will risk dilution of the trademark, which will tend to make the rights in the mark difficult to enforce. Thus, outside the distribution context, trademark licenses typically include very strong obligations of quality control, as well as the ability of the licensor to audit the quality of the products and to terminate the license easily for breach of minimum quality obligations.

This is a rough checklist for reviewing software license agreements. These issues focus on end user agreements, as opposed to distribution agreements.

Provision	Licensor	Licensee	Comments
Definition of Software	• Should specify object code only	• Should include updates	
License Grant	• Separate grants for each enumerated right of copyright • Non-transferable, non-sublicenseable, non-exclusive	• Patent license grant or non-assert • Irrevocable (see termination provisions) • Remember rights to perform, display, transmit • Include license grant to affiliates • Ability to run at outsourced data center	• Always define exclusivity.
Royalties	• Avoid resale price maintenance • Be sure license grants and royalties correspond • If royalties are a percentage (not a $ figure) or based on information known to licensee, include audit provision	• Royalties on net, not gross • Most favored nations (requires audit provision)	
Delivery	• No acceptance testing (causes revenue recognition problems)	• Include delivery obligation • Acceptance testing, with payment due only on acceptance	• Consider if this is really a development deal.
Maintenance and Support	• Efforts level to resolve errors: commercially reasonable • Escalation procedures • Including upgrades in license fees will cause revenue recognition problems • Ask for access to licensee's system via modem	• Lock in fees • Require maintenance for 3-5 years • Include updates, upgrades, error corrections • Ask for warranties that services are performed professionally • If service to be performed on site, as for insurance, indemnity for personal injury and employment related claims	• Access to source code doesn't mean you can fix problems; this requires technical expertise, often unique to the product.
Ownership	• Assignment of modifications • Reservation of rights • Reverse engineering prohibition (if object code)		• Licensees sometimes agree to assign back modifications to get the benefit of free support.

Provision	Licensor	Licensee	Comments
Bankruptcy	• Avoid defaults triggered by insolvency	• Recite application of 365(n) • Always file recordation of exclusive licenses • For object code licenses, include source code escrow	• Defaults triggered in a contract by bankruptcy (ipso facto clauses) are not enforceable.
Escrow	• Limit release conditions to cessation of business, cessation of maintenance services • Be aware of third party code to which you may have no source code rights • Licensee should pay escrow fees • Include dispute resolution procedure	• Release conditions should include any breach of maintenance, plus bankruptcy, insolvency • Present grant of rights, exercisable upon release • Include accelerated dispute resolution	
Warranties	• Include disclaimer of UCC implied warranties • Include limited remedies for breach of warranty • Do not give warranties of patent or trademark non-infringement	• "Naked" warranties (no disclaimer, limited remedies) • Performance warranty • Year 2000 warranty • Virus warranty • Non-infringement warranty • Corporate warranties	• Point of greatest contention in licenses.
Non-disclosure	• Non-disclosure and non-use • Source code should always be deemed confidential information	• Avoid non-use obligations • Residuals clause	• Always ask who will be disclosing more sensitive information. It's not always the licensor.
Term and Termination	• Bankruptcy (limited enforceability), insolvency, cessation of business • Accelerate termination due to non payment	• Termination at will • Irrevocable license = survives termination of agreement. No injunctive relief. • Adjudicated breach • Automatic cure by paying license fees	• One of the most important (and conceptually difficult) provisions. Consider what survives if the license terminates.
Indemnification	• Defend and settle 3rd party IP claims only • Ask for general indemnity from licensee	• Hold harmless for all damages, including licensee's costs, including consequential damages	• Always review in concert with limitations of liability.
Assignment	• Source code licenses should not be assignable	• Check assignment for problems in case of M&A transactions	• See license grant: "non-transferable."
Integration		• Some licensees like to integrate	

Provision	Licensor	Licensee	Comments
		documentation and sales literature, bids, RFPs	
Limitations of Liability	• Limit to fees paid • Include consequential damages for confidentiality breach	• No limits for indemnities, warranties	

NOTES

VIII: Week 7: Confidentiality and Non-Disclosure

Licensing agreements usually address the use and disclosure of confidential information through non-disclosure provisions. The structure of such provisions is closely linked with the principles of trade secret law. Trade secret law varies from state to state, but most states follow principles similar to those of the Uniform Trade Secrets Act.

Trade secret law is a hybrid of intellectual property law, contract law, and torts. Unlike patents and copyrights, trade secrets do not consist of an enumerated set of rights that are treated as property rights. Instead, trade secret "rights" derive from the ability to sue others for misappropriation, which the Uniform Trade Secret Act, Section 1 defines as "acquisition of a trade secret of another by a person who knows or has reason to know that the trade secret was acquired by improper means" or "disclosure or use of a trade secret of another without express or implied consent..." From this right of action follows the idea that the possessor of information must license others to use and disclose that information.

The 1990 Comment to Section 1 of the Uniform Trade Secret Act provides that proper means of acquisition of a trade secret include:

1. Discovery by independent invention;

2. Discovery by "reverse engineering";

3. Discovery under a license from the owner of the trade secret;

4. Observation of the item in public use or on public display;

5. Obtaining the trade secret from published literature.

This background of trade secret law explains much of the structure of typical non-disclosure provisions. Most non-disclosure agreements ("NDAs"), or non-disclosure provisions within other types of agreements, contain three essential elements: a definition of confidential information, a non-disclosure and non-use obligation, and an obligation to use at least reasonable efforts to maintain the secrecy of the information. For instance:

> "**Confidential Information**" means any information disclosed by either party to the other party, either directly or indirectly, in writing, orally or by inspection of tangible objects, which *is designated in writing as "Confidential," "Proprietary" or some similar designation* Information communicated orally will be considered Confidential Information *if such information is confirmed*

in writing as being Confidential Information within a reasonable time after the initial disclosure. Confidential Information will not, however, include any information that: (i) was publicly known and made generally available in the public domain prior to the time of disclosure by the disclosing party; (ii) becomes publicly known and made generally available after disclosure by the disclosing party to the receiving party through no action or inaction of the receiving party; (iii) is already in the possession of the receiving party at the time of disclosure by the disclosing party; (iv) is obtained by the receiving party from a third party without a breach of such third party's obligations of confidentiality; (v) is independently developed by the receiving party without use of or reference to the disclosing party's Confidential Information; or (vi) is required by law to be disclosed by the receiving party, provided that the receiving party gives the disclosing party prompt written notice of such requirement prior to such disclosure and assistance in obtaining an order protecting the information from public disclosure.

Non-use and Non-disclosure. Each party shall not use any Confidential Information of the other party for any purpose except to **[describe purpose]**. Each party shall not disclose any Confidential Information of the other party to third parties. Each party may disclose the other party's Confidential Information only to employees of such party who have a need to know such information to accomplish such purpose.

Maintenance of Confidentiality Each party shall take at least those measures that it takes to protect its own most highly confidential information, but in no event less than reasonable measures, to protect the secrecy of and avoid disclosure and unauthorized use of the Confidential Information of the other party.

Note that the exceptions to the definition loosely track the types of information that are not protectable as trade secrets. These exceptions are customary and rarely negotiated much. Note also the "writing requirement" in italics. Whether to include a writing requirement depends on the circumstances and the strategic position of your client. A writing requirement serves to limit the information that will be subject to the provision, so it favors the receiving party. Also, receiving parties justifiably argue that if there is no requirement to reduce the information to writing, they will not be able to control its use. Disclosing parties, also justifiably, argue that engineers and marketing personnel who discuss potential business initiatives do not tend to write down everything they discuss, so a writing requirement may not be inclusive enough. Each side is right, and this is sometimes a difficult issue to resolve.

The non-disclosure agreement is probably the one kind of agreement that, more than any other in the licensing practice, lends itself to the use of unadulterated forms. Stand-alone non-disclosure agreements are usually signed when two parties wish to conduct negotiations of a prospective business deal, to ensure that the information they disclose in the course of the negotiation is not used improperly, particularly if the deal is never executed. Most technology licensing agreements, though, include some form of confidentiality provision as part of the larger agreement. These provisions usually contain the "meat" of the non-disclosure agreement—the non-use and non-disclosure provisions.

The most important concept to understand about trade secrets is that reverse engineering is a defense to misappropriation. Therefore, it is sometimes possible to remove the "taint" by doing what is commonly referred to as a "clean room" development. This means that an entity that has been exposed to confidential information about a product, and is under and obligation to limit the information's use, can develop a similar product by performing the development using developers who have not been exposed to the information, in an environment that does not give them access to the information.

Nevertheless, matters of proof in trade secret infringement cases can be very difficult, because exposure to information is often not well documented. Therefore, many recipients of confidential information are reluctant to agree to any non-use provision without what is called a "residuals" clause. A residuals clause makes an exception—some would say a very large exception—to the non-use obligation by carving out of the actionable activities any inadvertent use of information. For example:

> **Residuals**. Nothing in this Agreement will be construed to prohibit a receiving party's employees from using Residuals as part of the employee's general skill or knowledge. As used herein, term "Residuals" means any Confidential Information retained in the memories of the receiving party's employees as a result of exposure to the disclosing party's Confidential Information.

Residuals clauses can be tricky to negotiate if the disclosing party is very concerned about reverse engineering of its products. However, these clauses are effective in reducing the exposure from taint. Alternatively, you may wish to simply remove the non-use obligation from the confidentiality terms, or only prohibit "willful" use.

One more point to remember about non-disclosure obligations is the remedy for breach. Many contracts contain limitations of liability that provide for exclusions of consequential damages. But to enter into a nondisclosure agreement or provision subject to such a limitation is unusual. This is because lost profits are available as damages for trade secret misappropriation, and indeed, constitute the principal area of damages for breach of a non-disclosure obligation. If your client's business associate discloses your client's secret information to a competitor of your client, the damages from the act of disclosure itself are minimal, and the loss of business due to the ability of that competitor to compete with the client is the principal form of harm. Thus, in any agreement where your client is disclosing sensitive information, you may wish to exclude breach of the non-disclosure provision from any disclaimer of consequential damages.

Doing Deals in the Web Space—Use and "Ownership" of Data

Drafting contracts for Web businesses requires an additional level of analysis to be applied to the confidentiality provisions of an agreement. In Web deals, the customer purchase history, viewing history, or demographic information arising from the use of a Web site may be one of the most important assets of the businesses involved. Customary confidentiality provisions such as the ones above do not adequately address this context, because they focus on information disclosed by one party to the other. In Web deals, much of the most valuable information is either generated automatically, or provided by the customer. Because of this, Web deals require additional terms regarding data use. Remember that absent a provision to the contrary, it is likely that each party can use or disclose customer information in any way it wishes. (There are some limitations, most notably COPPA. A discussion of on-line privacy is outside the scope of this section, but more information is available at http://www.privacyalliance.org/ (for the business side) and http://www.eff.org/privnow/ (for the consumer advocacy side).)

Your client will often couch this in terms of who "owns" the data or customers. But in legal terms, ownership of data is not very meaningful. While data collections enjoy some protection under copyright, that copyright is limited to the selection and organization of the data, and the copyright is considered "thin"—or easy to engineer around. (*Feist v. Rural Telephone Service*, 499 U.S. 340 (1991).) Remember that the important subject to focus on in the contract is not ownership, because merely stating who "owns" data will leave each party's position unclear and ripe for dispute, but the ability to use and disclose information. Here are some examples of how you might handle this issue in a Web deal. (For an example of a Web deal, see the "Co-Branding Agreement" form in the Forms Appendix.)

> **Registration Information**. The parties acknowledge that Service Provider will collect certain identifying information from users of the Co-Branded Service in the course of registering for the Co-Branded Service, or otherwise in the course of operating the Co-Branded Service, including without limitation contact name, address, email address, telephone, and credit card numbers ("Registration Information"). This sub-Section ___, and not the provisions of Section **[reference general confidentiality provision]** will apply to any Registration Information. Service Provider shall not disclose any Registration Information to any third party in individually identifiable form. For purposes of the foregoing, "individually identifiable form" (a) includes disclosure in a form where an individual datum that is unique to a user is disclosed, such as the distribution of customer lists or email lists; and (b) does not include the disclosure of data aggregated in such a way that a certain user's registration information can not be determined using reasonable efforts. Each party may use Registration Information **[to promote, develop, or enhance the Co-Branded Service][for any purpose],** however, neither party shall use the Registration Information to conduct direct mail, e-mail, or similar solicitations unless: (i) the other party agrees in advance in writing, including approval of the content any such solicitation (such approval not to be unreasonably withheld); and (ii) such use is consistent with the Co-Branded Service Privacy Policy (as defined below).
>
> **Service Provider Developed Information**. The parties acknowledge that Service Provider will develop information regarding users of the Co-Branded Service in the course of operating the Co-Branded Service, including without limitation cookies, user traffic data, preferences, and user transactional history ("Service Provider Developed Information"). This sub-Section ___, and not the provisions of Section **[reference general confidentiality provision]** will apply to Service Provider

Developed Information. Service Provider may use the Service Provider Developed information for any purpose and may disclose such information to third parties in its sole discretion. To the extent Service Provider discloses any Service Provider Developed Information to Company, Company may use such information for any purpose; however, Company shall not disclose such information, in individual or aggregate form, to any third party without Service Provider's prior written permission.

Privacy Policy. Notwithstanding anything to the contrary in this Section ___, each party shall use any Registration Information or Service Provider Developed Information only in accordance with any privacy policy posted on or promulgated to users in connection with the Co-Branded Service ("Co-Branded Service Privacy Policy"), and applicable law.

It is important, in the last clause, to limit uses to those in accordance with applicable law, because the trend in Web privacy law is accountability even more stringent than the privacy policies posted on a site.

Here is a checklist that you might find handy in reviewing non-disclosure agreements.

Non-Disclosure Agreement Checklist

PROVISION	FAVORS DISCLOSER	FAVORS RECIPIENT
Parties	• Recipient only; Discloser and affiliates	• Discloser only; Recipient and affiliates
Definition of Confidential Information	• Confidential Information broadly defined • specific types of information for the particular deal designated, without limitation, e.g., source code, software design • Confidential Information may also include information disclosed to Discloser by third parties.	• Confidential Information must be designated in writing • oral disclosures must be reduced to writing within 30 days • Confidential Information defined as specific types of information only • disclosure only with written consent of Recipient
Exceptions to Definition These exceptions are generally motivated by the limits of "misappropriation" in trade secret law.	• information publicly known or in the public domain prior to the time of disclosure • information publicly known after disclosure through no breach of Recipient • information already in the possession of Recipient without confidentiality restrictions • all above should be "as shown by contemporaneous written records of Recipient"	• information publicly known or in the public domain prior to the time of disclosure • information publicly known and made generally available after disclosure through no action or inaction of Recipient • information already in the possession of Recipient, without confidentiality restrictions • information obtained by the Receiver from a third party without a breach of confidentiality • information independently developed by the Receiver without use of Confidential Information
Non-Disclosure Covenant	• shall not disclose to any third party	• shall not disclose to any unrelated third party, • without Discloser's permission
Non-Use Covenant	• use only for designated purpose	• NO, or • use only for purposes of Agreement
Residuals	• none • If a residuals clause is unavoidable, should be limited to items remembered after return of documents or termination of the agreement.	• use of ideas, information and understandings retained in the memory of the Receiver's employees is allowed
Disclosure to Third Parties	• need to know basis only • employees must sign confidentiality agreement and be approved by Discloser • contractors must sign confidentiality agreement and be approved by Discloser • agreement must name Discloser as third party beneficiary	• disclosure upon court order or subpoena • disclosure to accountants, attorneys • disclosure to affiliates

PROVISION	FAVORS DISCLOSER	FAVORS RECIPIENT
	• disclosure upon court order or subpoena only if Discloser has opportunity to challenge • Recipient guarantees performance by independent contractors	
Degree of Care	• reasonable measures to protect against disclosure • at least those measures that Recipient takes to protect its own most highly confidential information. • immediate notice of any unauthorized use or disclosure	
Copying Restriction	• no copying except with Discloser's permission • must reproduce proprietary notices	
Reverse Engineering Restriction	• YES	• NO
Disclaimers	• implied warranty disclaimer • no obligation to proceed with business transaction	• no obligation to proceed with business transaction
Return of Materials	• return upon Discloser's request	• NO, or • return or destroy only upon termination
License	• disclaimer of implied license	
Term	• until Confidential Information falls into public domain	• as short as possible
Remedies	• Discloser entitled to injunctive relief	• limitation of liability, incidental and consequential damages • Discloser entitled to seek injunctive relief
Mutuality	• Recipient will disclose no confidential information	• reciprocal obligations

NOTES

IX: Week 8: Royalties

Drafting Payment Provisions

Payment provisions are some of the most difficult provisions to write in a contract. Particularly with payment provisions, you need to ensure that the language is drafted clearly and simply, because when contracts are performed by your client, a person with little or no legal training (such as a clerk or mid-level manager) may be tasked with examining the contract to determine the payments due. For this reason, I suggest drafting payment provisions using a contemporary style, by which I mean focusing on numbers rather than written language. For instance, here is an actual provision from a contract:

Customer shall contribute an amount equal to the construction costs per mile, multiplied by a fraction whose numerator shall be equal to the actual number of residences per cable-bearing strand foot and whose denominator shall be equal to fifteen (15) residences.

Remember that your clients are business people, and in technology businesses, they are often engineers. There is no reason to shy away from numerical exposition, which is much clearer.

Customer shall contribute an amount equal to $C \times RF/15$, where:

C = construction costs per mile

RF = actual number of residences per cable-bearing strand foot.

Lawyers add a lot of value when they make payment provisions precise. For instance, suppose your client is an application service provider that sells access to an on-line payment service, and charges based on the number of payments sent or received by the customer. Your client sends you a term sheet with the following payment term:

Initial Payment: $175,000

Transactions	Fee
0-100,000	$1
100,001-500,000	$.75
over 500,000	$.50

This level of detail is fairly common in term sheets, so you will have to fill in the blanks. Here are some of the questions you might ask your client:

- Is the initial payment due? *When the agreement is signed.*
- How often are the transactions fees paid? *Every quarter.*
- Is the initial payment recoupable against transaction fees? *Yes.* If so, what happens if the fees are not recouped? A refund? A credit? *There is no refund.*
- Will transactions be measured instantaneously or will they need to be reported in arrears? *Reported in arrears.*
- Will you invoice for the fees? *No.* If so, what are the payment terms?
- Are the tiers measured cumulatively? *They are measured separately.* For instance, if there are 150,000 transactions, do they all cost $.75, or are the first $100,000 billed at $1?

Here is how you might write this provision based on the italicized answers above:

4. **Fees**. In consideration of the rights granted herein, Licensee shall pay to Licensor the fees described in this Section 4.

4.1 **Initial Fee**. On or before the Effective Date, Licensee shall pay Licensor a non-refundable initial license fee of $175,000.

4.2 **Transaction Fees**. No later than 30 days after the end of each calendar quarter during the term of this Agreement, Licensee shall pay Licensor, for each transaction that occurs during such quarter, a transaction fee based on the cumulative number of transactions that have occurred during the term of this Agreement prior to the end of such quarter. Licensee may credit the amount paid by Licensee under Section 4.1 against cumulative amounts payable under this Section 4.2. Licensee shall deliver to Licensor, along with each payment, a report in reasonable detail showing the basis for such payment.

Transactions	Fee
0-100,000	$1
100,001-500,000	$.75
over 500,000	$.50

By way of example only, if 50,000 transactions have occurred prior to 3/1/01, and during the quarter 3/1/01 to 5/30/01, 250,000 transactions occur, then Licensee would pay to Licensor:

Payments for Q/E 2/28/01:	50,000 transactions @ $1 =	$ 50,000
Due for Q/E 5/30/01:	50,000 transactions @ $1 =	$ 50,000
	200,000 transactions @ $0.75 =	$150,000
Total:		$250,000
Less, initial payment:		($175,000)

Payment due for Q/E 5/30/01: $ 75,000

4.3 **Audits**. Licensee shall keep and maintain complete and accurate records of the transactions underlying the accounting statements to be furnished hereunder, and shall allow Licensor, or its representative, during office hours and at reasonable intervals, no more than once every six months to inspect and make extracts or copies of such records for the purpose of ascertaining the correctness of such statements. If any such examination and audit shall disclose any deficiency of 5% or more, Licensee shall pay, in addition to such deficiency, the costs of such examination and audit.

You may be wondering why the audit provision is included. Whenever the party receiving payment does not have access to the information necessary to confirm the accuracy of the payments, audits may be necessary.

Avoiding Antitrust Violations

A handful of antitrust issues come up in technology agreements—but by far the most frequent is resale price maintenance. To explain, we must examine the background law of antitrust. The following is a very brief summary of that law.

In the United States, there are both state and federal antitrust laws, but here we will focus on federal law, which is generally similar to state laws. Violation of antitrust law can mean four things: the appropriate authority (for instance, the Department of Justice) can bring a civil action against the violators, that authority can also institute a criminal prosecution against the violators, a member of the public or corporation who is harmed can bring a civil action against the violators, or a party to a contract containing a clause requiring anti-competitive practice can seek to avoid the contract or the anti-competitive portion of the contract. These remedies may be of interest to your clients especially because of the possible criminal penalties (which can extend to the officers or directors of a corporation) and because anti-competitive provisions in an agreement can be unenforceable.

The principal federal antitrust law is the Sherman Act, which has two sections. Section 2 of the Act prohibits operating a business as a monopoly. But for our purposes, Section 1 is more important: the section of the Sherman Act that prohibits certain anti-competitive practices. Anti-competitive practices are assessed in two groups: "*per se*" violations, i.e. practices that are always violations, and "rule of reason" violations, where the totality of the circumstances are assessed to determine if the practice is actually a violation.

Per se violations include, among others, price fixing, output restraints, and horizontal market division. These are all practices that are considered *per se* violations when engaged in by horizontal competitors. (Horizontal, in the antitrust sense, means between companies selling competing products in the same market. Vertical means between two links in the supply chain, such as a manufacturer and a distributor.) Thus, if a client sends you a term sheet that provides that parties that sell competing goods will meet to discuss the prices or output of their products on a quarterly basis, you should encourage your client to avoid agreeing to this at all—whether orally or in a written agreement. Many price fixing cases involve complex proof of whether an agreement actually existed. Do not assist the Department of Justice in sending your clients to prison by including it in a written agreement.

But the most common type of antitrust violation in a contract is not a horizontal restriction, but a vertical one: resale price maintenance. Resale price maintenance occurs, for example, when a manufacturer enters into an agreement with a reseller and sets a minimum price for the product. This has the anti-competitive effect of setting a floor for the price to the consumer, which means the reseller cannot compete with other resellers by lowering its prices. For example, suppose a publisher is paying a licensor a royalty of 10% of sales for a computer game. The game normally sells at $50, and the licensor wishes to receive no less than $5 per copy. However, setting a minimum price of $50 is clearly resale price maintenance.

This can usually be addressed by setting a minimum price between the licensor and the licensee. Thus, if the agreement should set the royalty at 10% of sale, but no less than $5 per copy, leaving the question of the retail price silent, or explicitly stating that the publisher can set any price it wishes, so long as it pays the $5 minimum. In fact, this will probably act to require the publisher to set a minimum price of $50, but if the publisher wishes, it can lower its prices to meet market conditions, if it is willing to absorb the additional relative cost of the royalty.

The other type of antitrust issue to watch out for in writing pricing provisions relates to the Robinson-Patman Act, which prohibits price discrimination in interstate sales of goods. This is one reason that licensors create classes of distributors such as OEMs and VARs; pricing to these kinds of distributors is usually lower than to a distributor that does not add value. Creating different classes gives a reasoned basis for different prices that might otherwise be viewed as price discrimination.

Patent Royalties

Royalties in patent licenses are generally written in a very specific way. Here is an example:

"**Licensed Product**" means any product within the scope of a Valid Claim or produced using any method within the scope of a Valid Claim.

"**Licensed Patents**" means the patent applications and patents listed on Exhibit A and all divisions, continuations, continuations-in-part, and substitutions thereof; all foreign patent applications corresponding to the preceding applications; and all U.S. and foreign patents issuing on any of the preceding applications, including extensions, reissues, and reexaminations.

"**Net Sales**" means revenues on an accrual basis, in accordance with U.S. generally accepted accounting principles (GAAP), as follows: the invoice price of Licensed Products sold by Licensee to third parties, less, to the extent included in such invoice price, the total of: (1) ordinary and customary trade discounts actually allowed; (2) credits, rebates and returns; (3) freight, postage, insurance and duties paid for and separately identified on the invoice, and (4) excise taxes, other consumption taxes, customs duties and compulsory payments to governmental authorities actually paid and separately identified on the invoice.

"**Valid Claim**" means (i) a claim of an issued and unexpired Licensed Patent that has not been held invalid in a final decision of a court of competent jurisdiction from which no appeal may be taken, and which has not been disclaimed or admitted to be invalid or unenforceable through reissue or otherwise, or (ii) a claim of a pending patent application within the Licensed Patents.

Royalties. Licensee shall pay to Licensor a royalty of __% on Net Sales of Licensed Products.

One Royalty. No more than one royalty payment will be due with respect to a sale of a particular Licensed Product. No multiple royalties will be payable because any Licensed Product, or its manufacture, sale or use is covered by more than one Valid Claim.

Royalty Term. Royalties due under this Section ___ will be payable on a country by country and Licensed Product by Licensed Product basis until *the expiration of the last to expire issued Valid Claim covering such Licensed Product* in such country, or if no such patent has issued in a country, until the **[third]** anniversary of the first commercial sale of a particular Licensed Product in such country.

This language is drafted to capture a royalty on products that are covered by a valid patent (with a three year grace period for the patents to issue). The underlined language seeks to avoid patent misuse by not charging for invalid claims, jurisdictions in which no valid patents issue, or expired patents. Sometimes, if the licensor is also licensing unpatented technology or know-how (sometimes called a "hybrid license" of patents and trade secrets), there is a reduction in royalties for products that are not, or are no longer, covered by a patent claim. Note that there are no multiple royalties for multiple patents. This is because the licensee's royalty rate should not be driven by the licensor's strategy in determining the breadth of each patent's claims.

Revenue Recognition

For software licensing agreements, you should also be aware of the recent rules for revenue recognition. In October, 1997, the American Institute of Certified Public Accountants (AICPA), which promulgates the rules used by financial auditors to review the financial records of corporations, issued a set of new rules for revenue recognition for software licensing. (Statement of Position 97-2.) Under these rules, revenue cannot be recognized or "booked" until it is free of contingencies or other obligations that might make it likely that the licensor would be obligated or likely to give the licensee a refund. This issue comes up most frequently within the context of negotiating remedies for the licensee if the software does not perform properly; most licensees insist on a refund if this happens during the warranty period for the product—usually one to three months. But if a refund is available, the licensor cannot book the revenue for the license until the warranty period has expired. These are examples of the type of provision that would result in a contingency, and thus make the licensor unable to book revenue until after the warranty period.

Acceptance. Upon delivery of the Software, Licensee will have the right to evaluate the Software. When Licensee has made a finding as to whether the Software is in accordance with the applicable specifications, it will promptly provide a written acceptance or rejection to Licensor. In the event Licensee has not provided a written notice of rejection within ____ days after delivery of the Software, the Software will be deemed accepted. Any notice of rejection shall set forth in reasonable detail the basis for the rejection. Upon receipt of a written notice of rejection, Licensor shall **[promptly] [within ____ days]** submit a corrected version of the Software, and the Software will again be subject to the acceptance procedure described above. In the event Licensee rejects the Software, Licensee may, in its sole discretion and immediately upon written notice, terminate this Agreement, *and Licensor shall refund all fees previously paid by Licensee.*

Performance Warranty. Licensor warrants that during the period 90 days after the Effective Date, the Software will function in accordance with the specifications for the Software and applicable documentation. In the case of a breach of the warranty in this Section ____, Licensor shall promptly repair or replace nonconforming Software. If the Software is not corrected to Licensee's reasonable satisfaction within ____ days, Licensee may, in its sole discretion and immediately upon written notice, terminate this Agreement, and *Licensor shall refund all fees previously paid by Licensee.*

In each case, the refund creates a contingency, during the period in which the refund is available. In addition, if a license obligates a licensor to deliver a specific update or new version of the software, the licensor may be unable to book a portion of the license fee until it is delivered.

Payment Terms and INCOTERMS

Royalty provisions generally also include a recitation of payment terms. To review agreements with payment terms, you will need to understand some business nomenclature:

Net 30. The amount of the invoice is due in 30 days.

2% net 10. If the payment is made within 10 days, the payor can deduct a 2% discount.

FOB ("Free on Board"). If a product will be delivered "FOB Seller's facility" then the buyer pays for freight and shipping from the Seller's facility to it own premises.

"FOB" and similar terms are defined in the publication INCOTERMS, which is a set of standard trade definitions used in international sales contracts published by the International Chamber of Commerce. (http://www.iccwbo.org/index_incoterms.asp.) Terms such as "FOB," "CIF" and "Ex Works" are shorthand terms that define, for products that are bought and sold, which party (the buyer or seller) will pay freight, insurance, and the like, and where title will transfer. You need not use these shorthand terms if you spell out when title transfers and who bears the various expenses of shipment and risk of loss. But you should be familiar with these terms when you run across them.

NOTES

X: Week 9: Bankruptcy and Escrows

Continuation of Rights

Licensees usually worry about one thing more than any other—ensuring that their right to use licensed intellectual property will not end unexpectedly. If a license ends, the licensee is suddenly required to cease using technology that is covered by a license, and can be subject to injunction if it fails to do so. The issue of ensuring a licensee's continued ability to use licensed technology is similar to the idea of "quiet enjoyment" in real property law. Someone who has paid for the use of property wants to be able to engage in that use undisturbed.

In a sense, the threat of injunction against the use of unlicensed technology makes all other issues secondary, because if the licensed intellectual property is important enough, an injunction can force a licensee to stop its business. Even if we reduce this to a question of money, licensees can incur significant expenses in engineering around technology they can no longer use. But no amount of money may be able to save a business that loses time-to-market advantage, or whose sales or operations suddenly cease, because of an unexpected re-engineering problem.

In contrast, if a license ends at the end of its natural term, the licensee knows in advance it will have to re-engineer around the licensed technology. It must take steps so that the licensed technology is no longer needed, or enter into a renewed license, or license substitute technology from another licensor. If the date of termination of the license is known, the licensor can plan for the costs associated with these technology initiatives.

Licensees usually must live with the risk that they will lose their rights if they breach the terms of their license agreement, and they can manage this risk by being careful to abide by its terms. But most licensees have little or no control over one event that may cause a license to terminate—the failure of the licensor's business.

To understand why this is such a significant issue, we need to understand some basics of bankruptcy law. It is worth nothing that many companies go out of business without entering into formal federal bankruptcy proceedings. Nevertheless, the intricacies of federal bankruptcy law govern how we draft the portions of license agreements that address this issue of quiet enjoyment.

Bankruptcy Law Summary

Bankruptcy law exists to give debtors a fresh start when they cannot pay their debts or service them. The law of bankruptcy is largely federal law, though there are also state laws that are similar to federal bankruptcy law. The Bankruptcy Code was enacted in 1978, and is codified in Chapter 11 of the United States Code.

When a debtor wishes to cease doing business and liquidate his assets, he may avail himself of Chapter 7 of the Bankruptcy Code or "straight bankruptcy." After a petition under Chapter 7 is filed, a trustee is appointed by the bankruptcy court and a bankruptcy estate is created that consists of the assets of the debtor. The trustee has the power to dispose of the assets owned by the estate. Under Chapter 7, the trustee converts the assets to cash, or "liquidates" them, and then distributes the cash proceeds to the creditors. The creditors must accept whatever assets are distributed to them by the trustee in accordance with Chapter 7. This is called a discharge of debts. This discharge is what gives the debtor a fresh start.

> **Example**: Bill owes Michael $50,000. Bill files a petition under Chapter 7. The receiver liquidates Bill's assets and only receives $15,000 for the assets, which he pays to Michael. If Bill receives a discharge, Michael will not be able to pursue Bill for the remaining $35,000.

Chapter 11 is different kind of bankruptcy petition that involves the reorganization or rehabilitation of the debtor's assets, rather than a liquidation. A debtor corporation may file a petition under Chapter 11 if it wishes to restructure its financial obligations so that it may continue to operate, provide its employees with jobs, pay its creditors, and ultimately, produce a return for its stockholders. Like a Chapter 7 petition, the Chapter 11 petition results in the appointment of a trustee; however, the trustee works with management to restructure the business and repay the creditors, most likely from revenue generated after the restructuring. This kind of petition takes advantage of the value of the debtor entity as a going concern, which would be lost in a liquidation.

In Chapter 11, the trustee has the power to accept or reject any executory contract to which the debtor is a party. (See Bankruptcy Code Section 365(a).) An executory contract is any contract that is currently being performed. If the debtor is a developer of intellectual property, it is likely to be party to many executory licensing contracts. For example, a software agreement may involve an up-front license fee that results in a perpetual license. The obligations of the licensor may be limited to little more than providing the grant of license, or may include some maintenance obligations. If the debtor uses such a business model, it is likely to have many executory contracts in place upon the filing of a Chapter 11 petition.

However, the ability of the trustee to reject a license agreement would mean that the licensee would unexpectedly lose its quiet enjoyment, through no fault of the licensee. To remedy this business problem, and to make the treatment of licensees of bankrupt companies fairer, Section 365(n) was enacted.

One other rule of bankruptcy law is important to license agreements: the *ipso facto* rule. Provisions in agreements that allow termination of the agreement or any other modification of the debtor's rights under the agreement are unenforceable once a petition has been filed, because they would compromise the value of the bankruptcy estate. (See Bankruptcy Code Sections 541(c)(1); 365(e).)

Section 365(n)

Congress enacted 365(n) of the Bankruptcy Code (the Intellectual Property Bankruptcy Act) in 1988. Section 365(n) provides two options for the licensee in the event that a licensor's trustee rejects a license in connection with a bankruptcy petition. The first option, under § 365(n)(1)(A), allows the licensee to treat the license as terminated, cease exercising the license, and file a creditor claim against the bankruptcy estate for damages in connection with breach of the licensing contract. The other option, under § 365(n)(1)(B), allows the licensee to retain its rights to exercise the license for the term of the agreement. The licensee must continue to make royalty payments to the licensor. Conversely, the licensor is freed from any obligations under the license—such as maintenance or support—other than the grant of rights itself.

Section 365(n) is by no means a panacea for the licensee. First, although 365(n) is drafted as covering licenses of "intellectual property," that term does not include trademarks, trade names or service marks. Thus, a trademark licensee cannot benefit by it. Also, the payment of royalties required to continue enjoyment of the license is construed broadly. (*In re Prize Frize*, 32 F.3d 426 (9th Cir. 1994).) if the contract includes payments other than royalties, the licensee must be careful to characterize the consideration for these payments properly. Otherwise, the licensee will have a continuing obligation to pay all "royalties," whereas the licensor will no longer be obligated to perform obligations covered by them. For instance, many software agreements include free maintenance and support for the license fee. Under 365(n), all of the fee would likely be considered a royalty.

Escrows: Access to Source Code and Technology

Some, but not all, computer programs are written in programming languages that are "compiled." This means that the program executed by the computer is not actually the text written by the programmer. Here is why: computer processors, the electronics that actually make the computer perform operations, do not process text. They speak in their own language of "binary" code—a stream of 1's and 0's that flow through the processor chip of the computer in the form of positive and negative electrical charges that are set and re-set within the materials that compose the chip. To make the computer processor chip understand what to do, the text written by the programmer has to be translated into binary language.

The text written by the programmer is like a word processing file. It might look like this:

int i, j, k;

printf ("THIS PROGRAM ADDS TWO NUMBERS:\n");

printf ("PLEASE ENTER THE FIRST NUMBER:");

scanf ("%d",&i);

printf ("PLEASE ENTER THE SECOND NUMBER:");

scanf ("%d",&j);

k = j + i;

printf ("THE SUM OF %d AND %d IS %d.", i, j, k);

The programmer, finished writing her program, saves this text to a file. This file is called a "source code" file. Then, she runs the translation program, which is called a "compiler." The compiler translates the text above into a stream of 1's and 0's that tells the computer lots of information based on the text. Obviously, the computer needs to create in memory places to store the changing values of the variables i, j and k. But the compiler also needs to tell the processor other information. For instance, the "scanf" and "printf" statements allow input and output on the computer screen. The processor needs to know where to find the information coming from the keyboard, how to translate the text from the keyboard (e.g. "2") to a number value to assign to the variable, where to display the information, etc. This is accomplished by assigning certain locations, called "addresses," to the keyboard and display screen, and interpreting the numeral "2" as the number 2.

If this is confusing, don't worry. All you need to understand is that each line of the text above needs to be translated to multiple lines of binary instructions that the computer processor can execute. These binary instructions are stored in a different file, called an "object code" file or a "binary."

When you buy a program for your computer, chances are that you are buying object code. Your computer has no trouble understanding object code. But you cannot understand it. You cannot see the original programming text, because you do not have access to the source code.

Now imagine that there is an error (a "bug") in your program. But you only have object code, not source code. Even if you are a programmer and have the skill to de-bug and fix the problem, you cannot, because you would need to modify the source code and create a new object code file. Now further imagine that you are a licensee, and the licensed software is your payroll processing system, and the licensor, whom you have relied upon for three years to provide technical support when you have bugs, has just entered Chapter 7. You are in trouble.

The customary answer to this problem is called a source code escrow. An independent trustee—usually a firm in the business of doing technology escrows—is appointed as the escrow agent for licensor and licensee. The parties enter into a 3-way agreement that is essentially a trust arrangement. The licensor delivers a copy of the source code to the escrow agent, and is usually required to deliver a source code update whenever it delivers a corresponding object code update to the licensee under the agreement. Upon occurrence of a triggering event, the escrow agent delivers the escrowed source code to the licensee. The escrow agreement, or the original license agreement, should include a license grant that is effective upon delivery by the escrow agent.

Most of the provisions of escrow agreements are not heavily negotiated. Sometimes the parties negotiate who will pay the fees. Typically the licensee pays these fees, if only because a licensor nearing bankruptcy may not place escrow fees at the top of its financial priorities, and the escrow agent may not be willing to release an escrow deposit with fees due in arrears. Parties also negotiate the dispute resolution mechanism if there is a disagreement over whether a triggering event has occurred. Licensees tend to want fast arbitration, because obtaining the source code a year after a bug has appeared and maintenance has ended does not do much to address the licensee's quiet enjoyment issue.

The heavily negotiated provisions are the trigger events. Some of them relate to bankruptcy, and some do not. They range as follows:

- Filing of Chapter 7 (also cessation of business in the ordinary course, liquidation without filing of a bankruptcy provision). This trigger is ubiquitous and seldom controversial.
- Filing of Chapter 11. The licensor may argue that, for the reasons discussed above, Chapter 11 will not be likely to interrupt maintenance services.
- Breach of the License's Maintenance Obligations. Licensors are wary of agreeing to this, particularly if the maintenance obligations in the agreement are vague or stringent.
- Change of Control of Licensor. This is a "poison pill" for an acquisition of the licensor, and the licensor usually tries to negotiate against it.

When drafting and negotiating licenses that involve escrows, the parties may attach an executed escrow agreement as an exhibit to the document. However, the parties often do not have time to set up the escrow or have the escrow agent sign the document before executing the license itself. In those cases, you might use the following provision, which is drafted to favor the licensor:

> **Escrow**. No later than 30 days after the Effective Date, the parties shall enter into a source code escrow agreement with **[an escrow agent reasonably acceptable to both parties][name escrow agent]**, pursuant to which Licensor shall make Licensee the beneficiary of source code and source materials embodying the Software that are deposited by Licensor with such agent. Licensor hereby grants to Licensee the right to use, reproduce, and prepare derivative works of the source code and source materials for the Software and derivative works thereof; provided that Licensee may exercise such rights only in the event of a release of such materials pursuant to such source code escrow agreement, and only for the purpose of maintaining and correcting errors in the Software. The parties agree that such release will take place only if and when Licensor ceases business in the ordinary course. Licensee shall pay all fees associated with such escrow account.

Note the present language of grant in the license: "Licensor *hereby* grants to Licensee...provided that Licensee may exercise such rights only in the event of a release of such materials pursuant to such source code escrow agreement." This is the proper way to draft this provision, as opposed to: "Licensor *shall grant* to Licensee... upon a release of such materials pursuant to such source code escrow agreement." This is an issue for the licensee's counsel to spot. The obligation to grant a license is difficult to enforce, because courts are reluctant to grant positive injunctions; i.e. injunctions requiring affirmative steps, because courts do not want to be in a continuing position of evaluating the enjoined party's performance of the injunction. They prefer to grant negative injunctions, i.e. injunctions prohibiting activities, or to simply award legal relief, i.e. damages, because it is easier to prove or disprove compliance with the injunctive order. Thus, it is difficult for a licensee to enforce a covenant to grant rights. Therefore, the licensee prefers a grant of a "springing" right, so there is no question that the license can be exercised without a court order.

The Flow-Down Problem

Escrows are so ubiquitous now that it is easy to forget the due diligence your client must do to make sure it has the right to make source code available and grant the kind of licenses it must grant to effectuate an escrow. Few software developers develop their entire product from scratch. Take the hypothetical example of Thumbelina and Fair Share. Many of Fair Share's customers want an escrow of source code in the event Fair Share goes out of business. But most of the software provided by Fair Share to its customers belongs to licensors like Thumbelina. Absent an agreement for that purpose, Fair Share cannot grant its customers any rights in Thumbelina's source code. If its did, then in the type of escrow provision described above, a failure of the business of Fair Share would trigger release of the source code of Thumbelina. Thumbelina is likely to take a dim view of this.

If this problem arises, one way to solve it is as follows, where Fair Share is Licensee and Thumbelina is Licensor:

> If Licensee is in material breach of its support obligations for the Software to any customer of Licensee to whom Licensee has licensed the Software under this Agreement, Licensor shall, at its sole option and discretion, either (1) assume Licensee's rights and obligations for support of the Software with respect to such customer, including without limitation making such customer the beneficiary of and granting such customer the rights in Software source code and source materials of this Section ___, or (2) instruct the escrow agent to release the source code and source materials to such customer, and grant to such customer the right to use, reproduce, prepare derivative works of, perform, display and transmit the source code and source materials for the Software and derivative works thereof.

This will address the customer's need for continuing access to technology, but not force Thumbelina to lose control of its source code.

NOTES

XI: Week 10: Selected Topics on International Licensing

This chapter describes some of the issues that come up most frequently in "international deals"—which means deals between your U.S. client and an entity outside the United States. It is important for you to understand, and for you to advise your client, that it is not possible for a United States lawyer to spot every issue that might arise under an international agreement. Although the law of countries with a British-based legal system (or "common law" system) tend to share common principles that may allow you to spot issues in international agreements, you and your client will be best served by hiring local counsel to review any international agreement. Local counsel can be instructed to review the document only for issues of local law, and to suggest changes to maximize enforceability in local jurisdictions. Clients sometimes elect to forego this additional review in the interest of cost control, but you should always suggest it.

With that in mind, here are some—but of course not all—of the issues that arise most frequently in international deals.

Distributors and Sales Agents

The most common unexpected result from international agreements is running afoul of local laws regarding sales agents and distributors. Some nations have enacted laws that make it difficult to terminate agreements with distributors or sales agents—particularly exclusive appointees—without reimbursing the costs of market development. Some attorneys handle this by adding a provision such as:

> **Limitation of Liability upon Termination**. The parties acknowledge that Manufacturer will not be liable to Representative for any damages arising from termination by either party of this Agreement in accordance with its terms, including without limitation any damages for lost profits or business, compensation for expenses related to the development of business, branding, or goodwill.

In fact, local courts may simply ignore such provisions, and there may be little that can be done in the text of the agreement to address this issue. Laws protecting distributors and sales agents are based on public policy protecting the local entities, and contracting out of them may not be possible.

Antitrust and the E.U.

For deals involving E.U. member nations, you need to be cognizant of local antitrust law. Article 81 takes a somewhat different approach from the United States' Sherman Act, in that it globally prohibits agreements in restraint of trade with some exceptions. Article 81(1) prohibits agreements that appreciably restrict or distort competition. Like the Sherman Act and Robinson-Patman Act, it covers agreements that fix prices, limit production, allocate markets, or apply "dissimilar conditions to equivalent transactions with other trading parties…" Agreements between small and medium-sized enterprises ("SMEs," which have 250 or fewer employees, and fall below certain minimum levels or revenue and assets that are revised periodically.) are not covered because they are not capable of appreciably affecting trade between E. U. member states. In addition, Article 81(3) renders the prohibition inapplicable to agreements with sufficient benefits to outweigh anti-competitive effects. There are also block exemptions that may apply. A full discussion of Article 81 is beyond the scope of this book, but you should be aware that for any agreement with a member nation, you should seek review by local counsel for compliance with Article 81. (More information is available at http://europa.eu.int/comm/competition/publications/rules_en.pdf.)

Differences in Intellectual Property Law

Of course, it is not possible to list all of the differences between United States intellectual property laws and the intellectual property laws of other nations. However, you should be generally aware of some of the differences, so you can spot issues in advance. Some of them are:

- First-to-file patent and trademark systems.
- Limitations on patentable subject matter (e.g. medical procedures and biological products).
- Limitations on enforceability of reverse engineering prohibitions.
- More stringent "Moral Rights" for copyrightable works.
- Differences in effect of joint ownership.
- Copyright coverage of databases.
- Local laws on the use or export of personal information.
- Differences in enumerated rights under patent and copyright.
- Limited enforceability of grant-backs.

Withholding Tax

Many nations have tax treaties with the United States that require the withholding of amounts from certain types of income, such as royalty income. Where this is the case, the withholding percentage usually ranges from 5% to 15%. In a case where the licensor is a United States entity and the licensee is in Japan, for instance, the licensee must withhold 10% of royalty income and pay it to the government of Japan as an income tax, paid for the benefit of the United States company. Think of this as similar to the withholding that takes place for your own wage income—it is deducted from monies owed to you. By virtue of the treaty between Japan and the United States, Japan will issue a certificate as proof of this withholding, and the United States licensor can deduct this amount from taxes payable in the United States.

This sounds fine on its face. But some licensors, particularly start-ups, may not owe any corporate income taxes because they are not yet profitable. The credits may only be carried forward for a limited time. In addition, only certain sources of income may qualify for the deduction. Therefore, your client should be sure that it is able to use the tax credit, before it agrees to set the royalty rate. Otherwise, the deduction may effectively reduce the royalties paid by 10%.

Here are the provisions you might use to effectuate a royalty with a deduction, or without deduction (the latter being called a "gross-up" clause).

> **Taxes**. Licensee may withhold from payment made to Licensor under this Agreement any income taxes required to be withheld by Licensee under the laws of **[the United States]**. If any tax is withheld by Licensee, Licensee shall provide Licensor receipts or other evidence of such withholding and payment to the appropriate tax authorities.
>
> **Gross Payments**. All payments by Licensee must be made free and clear of, and without reduction for, any and all taxes, including without limitation sales, use, property, license, value added, excise, franchise, incomes, withholding or similar taxes. Any such taxes that are otherwise imposed on payments to Licensor shall be the sole responsibility of Licensee. Licensee shall provider Licensor with official receipts issued by the appropriate taxing authority of such other evidence as is reasonably requested by Licensor to establish that such taxes have been paid.

Dispute Resolution and Selection of Governing Law

Dispute resolution methods tend to be handled differently in international deals. In international deals, it is far more common to use arbitration, and far more common to pick a neutral or "half-way" site for the arbitration to be held. In international deals, neither side generally feels comfortable giving the other side a "home-court advantage" by using the courts of the other side's country. Also, a company with no assets in a particular country may be effectively judgment-proof because the assets are unreachable by that country's courts. There is no particular reason for the Japanese government, for instance, to enforce a judgment of a United States court. Arbitration awards, in contrast, can be enforced through an arbitration treaty called the New York Convention (information at http://arbiter.wipo.int/arbitration/ny-convention/), to which many nations adhere—but the process of actually executing a judgment can be long and expensive. Still, in international deals, arbitration is usually considered the only reasonable choice. The site of arbitration is usually a large city with vigorous business activities and appropriate language and location—such as London or Geneva for deals involving European entities, and Honolulu or Tokyo for deals involving Asian entities. Always remember to specify the site and language for any arbitration.

Export Restrictions

In most international agreements, some goods, money or technology will travel across national borders. This makes the transaction subject to relevant export laws. Here is an example of an export clause in an international agreement:

> **U. S. Export Control**. Distributor acknowledges that Manufacturer is subject to regulation by agencies of the United States, such as the U.S. Department of Commerce, which prohibit export of certain products or technology to certain countries or nationals of certain countries. Manufacturer's obligations to provide the Software are subject to any applicable United States laws and regulations applicable to the provision of technology or products, including without limitation the Export Administration Act of 1979. Distributor shall cooperate with Manufacturer to obtain any export licenses that Manufacturer reasonably believes necessary to effectuate the supply of the Software hereunder. Distributor shall comply with all such applicable laws and regulations.

Obviously, inserting such a clause may make little difference in the legal liability of either party. It is highly unlikely that the manufacturer could be compelled to violate the law, or to pay damages for failing to do so. But this type of clause may assist the manufacturer in enforcing export restrictions against a distributor that is entirely outside the reach of U.S. law and courts, and perhaps more important, if the export laws are broken by the distributor, this type of clause may provide the manufacturer with evidence of its own efforts to try to comply with the law—thus avoiding any fines or culpability that may arise from willful violation of them.

As a corollary, the transfer of money across national boundaries can raise issues. Currency controls may make it difficult to exchange currencies or make cross-border payments. This may be addressed with a provision such as the following:

> **Currency Control**. Licensee represents and warrants that no currency control laws in effect during the term of this Agreement will prevent the payment to Licensor of any amounts due hereunder. In the event that any such laws come into effect, Licensee shall immediately notify Licensor, and Licensor may, at its sole option and discretion: (a) require Licensee to deposit all amounts due for Licensor's account in a local bank; or (b) terminate this Agreement.

Also remember, when writing payment terms, that you will have to set an exchange rate for currencies, and properly denominate the currency units in which payment are expressed. Don't forget that "dollars" can be ambiguous, so use "U.S. dollars," if that is what you mean.

Language Clauses

Finally, in any agreement where the two sides are from areas that speak different languages, agreements are likely to be translated into both languages. You should clarify which language is the official, controlling version. Here is an example of a language selection clause:

> **Language**. This Agreement is in the English language only, which language will be controlling in all respects, and all versions hereof in any other language will not be binding on the parties hereto. All communications and notices to be made or given pursuant to this Agreement must be in the English language.

Needless to say, if the official language of the agreement is German, and you do not speak German, and are reviewing an English translation, your client needs to engage local counsel to work with you. Even if you have a conversational knowledge of the official language, you may not understand the nuances of meaning that are so important in legal agreements.

NOTES

XII: Week 11: Warranties, Indemnities and Limitations of Liability

Allocation of risk provisions—warranties, indemnities, and limitations of liability—are the provisions that send most clients, and even some lawyers, into a mental tailspin. Of all the provisions in transactional agreements, they are the most densely written, the farthest removed from immediate business deal, and the most difficult to analyze. This section is a crash course on how to understand, write, and negotiate these provisions. It focuses on the use of these provisions in intellectual property licenses.

Warranty

First, what is a warranty? Contracts are composed of promises, or "covenants." For instance: "Licensee shall pay the Licensor the sum of $250,000 on or before January 1, 2001." If Licensee does not pay, Licensee has breached the covenant. A warranty is simply a covenant that a particular fact is true. If the fact is not true, the party making the warranty has breached the warranty. For instance:

"Corporate Representations"

Representations and Warranties. Licensor hereby represents and warrants that:

(a) it has the right to enter into this Agreement; it is a corporation duly organized, validly existing, and in good standing under the laws of the state of its incorporation; it has the corporate power and authority for, and has by all necessary corporate action authorized, the execution and delivery of this Agreement, and the performance of its obligations hereunder; and

(b) the execution, performance and delivery of this Agreement by Licensor does not conflict with, or constitute any default under, any contract, agreement or other obligation of Licensor.

The first clause is often called a "corporate warranty," because it focuses on corporate formalities. The second, implicitly, focuses on exclusivity and non-competition covenants, because these are the easiest to breach by entering into an agreement. So, if this is a license of software, and Licensor has already granted an exclusive license to another licensee, the warranty is breached.

In theory, because a warranty constitutes a statement of fact, it should be associated with a particular moment in time, for instance, when the agreement becomes effective (as in the example above), or during an explicit warranty period. Otherwise, it may be hard to determine if the warranty is true. For instance:

Performance Warranty. Licensor warrants to Licensee that, for 90 days following the first delivery of the Software, the Software will perform in all material respects in accordance with its applicable published specifications.

Although this warranty is forward-looking, it is confined to a particular time. It is called a "performance warranty" because it focuses on the way a particular piece of technology performs. This is why warranties in technology agreements are complicated: they must address not only what a licensed thing is, but how it works. Thus, in the real world of contract drafting, and particularly in intellectual property licenses, warranties are often written as continuing obligations. For instance:

Non-Infringement Warranty. Licensor hereby represents and warrants to Licensee that the Software does not and will not infringe any third party's copyright, patent, trade secret, or trademark rights.

This is sometimes called a "non-infringement warranty" or "intellectual property warranty." What is the difference between warranting that software is non-infringing for the whole term of the agreement, or the Licensor making a covenant to get the necessary licenses to cause the software not to infringe? Not much. This warranty's indefinite, forward-looking nature makes it hard to distinguish from a covenant. But covenants like this are called warranties for strategic drafting reasons—which will become apparent as you read further.

Indemnities

What is an indemnity? Insurance companies are in the business of selling indemnities. When you make an indemnity by contract, you are acting like an insurer. If something goes wrong, you pay money or take certain actions to make it right. For instance:

Indemnity For Breach of Warranty. Licensor shall defend, indemnify and hold harmless Licensee from and against all third party costs, liability, claims, loss, damages, expenses or judgments arising out of any breach of any warranty made by the Licensor pursuant to Section ___ (Warranties).

Now, you can see why some lawyers love to call covenants "warranties" and put them in the warranty section. It is customary to indemnify for any breach of warranty; less so to indemnify for a breach of every covenant of the agreement. So, re-characterizing covenants as warranties can expand the scope of the indemnities of a contract.

Many people are confused by the language "defend, indemnify, and hold harmless." There is no generally accepted difference between "indemnifying" and "holding harmless." While case law varies on the subject, *Black's Law Dictionary* defines these terms in essentially the same way. Each requires the indemnitor to bear the costs that arise from a particular event, such as a lawsuit by another party. Defending is the obligation to hire counsel to appear in court and defend a lawsuit. Thus, if the Licensor is only obligated to indemnify, it may be that the Licensee must hire counsel to defend a suit brought against it. If the Licensor is also obligated to defend, then the Licensor has to hire lawyers and appear in court—not just reimburse the Licensee for its costs in doing so.[vii]

Now, take a look at the following provision, which is more favorable to the Licensor:

"Defend and Settle Provision"

Obligation to Defend Third Party Claims. Licensor shall defend, or at its option settle, all lawsuits, actions, claims, or demands ("Claims") against Licensee, and shall pay any associated third party damages, liabilities, judgments, and costs (including court costs) and fees (including attorneys' fees) arising therefrom, to the extent such Claims arise out of any breach of any warranty made by the Licensor under Section ___ (Warranties).

This is not an obligation to indemnify or hold harmless—only an obligation to defend and pay the resulting damages. What is the difference?

Think about what you get when you buy insurance. Suppose you purchase a disability policy and a malpractice policy. The disability policy is more like an obligation to "hold harmless." If you become disabled and have to stop working, even if the disability is cause by illness, or an unknown cause, and not by another person, your insurer will pay you money to help compensate you for this. The malpractice policy is more like a defend/settle agreement. If a client sues you for malpractice, the insurer will hire lawyers to defend you and pay any malpractice damages awarded to the plaintiff. Will you get any money from your insurer because you get sued for malpractice? No, the plaintiff gets it. Will any third party get your salary during the period of disability? No, you get it.

The example above shows an attempt (by the Licensor) to reduce the Licensor's exposure for indemnity claims. In contrast, the following provision is a very broad indemnity, an attempt to expand liability:

General Indemnity

Indemnity. Licensor shall defend, indemnify and hold harmless Licensee from and against all costs, liability, claims, losses, damages, expenses or judgments arising out of any act or omission of Licensor, or any breach of any representation, warranty or covenant of Licensor in this Agreement.

This provision covers—or the Licensee could reasonably claim it covers—all of the following, and more:

- a tort that is Licensor's fault (which is an "act or omission" of Licensor)
- a claim of intellectual property infringement (which would be caused by an omission of the Licensor to secure the necessary licenses to prevent infringement)
- an intentional act by a Licensor employee harming a Licensee employee (such as sexual harassment)
- a breach of the agreement
- a breach of a warranty

Note that the "act or omission" in this provision is not expressly required to be related to the subject matter of the agreement. In effect, Licensor is now in the business of insuring the Licensee against many different forms of harm or claim. Thus, indemnities can be very specific or very broad, and can result in significant exposure, and this is why they are sometimes so hotly negotiated.

Limitations of Liability

When people have difficulty understanding limitations of liability, it is usually because they do not understand the liabilities that arise from breach of a contract in the first place. So, it is worthwhile to go through a quick recap of remedies law. When you, as a party to a contract, make an agreement, it results in a benefit to the other party—the so-called "benefit of the bargain." If you breach your promise, you mast pay "compensatory damages"—damages that compensate the other party for losing the benefit of the bargain. These are also called "direct damages."

There are different ways to calculate the amount of direct damages. For instance, imagine a contract for the sale of semiconductor chipsets where the seller, ChipCo, agrees to sell chipsets to LapTopCo. However, ChipCo refuses to sell the chipsets to LapTopCo, breaching its promise. ChipCo would have to pay LapTopCo the difference between the amount LapTopCo had to pay to replace the chipsets on the open market and the price ChipCo had agreed to accept. If LapTopCo instead refuses to buy the chipsets, then ChipCo can sell the chipsets on the open market, and recover the difference between the (presumably lower) price it gets for them, and the amount LapTopCo agreed to pay. As you can see, these "costs of cover" damages are straightforward, easy to calculate, and subject to mitigation—or the requirement of the damaged party to try to sell or buy replacement goods to minimize the money it lost. There are other ways to measure damages, too, but they are generally based on the economic value of the bargain, not the enjoyment or "utility" value the performance of the contract might have conferred.

Other types of damages include incidental damages, punitive damages, and consequential damages. Incidental damages are, as the name suggests, typically minimal, and punitive damages are not generally awarded in breach of contract suits. (Equitable relief such as injunctions or TROs are also available, but this discussion is about damages, so we will set questions of equity aside.) So we are left with the most important: consequential damages.

Consequential damages come from the old English case law homily *Hadley v. Baxendale* The rule is that a party who breaches a contract is liable for all damages that he knew or should have known would result from his breach. Therefore, if you are the licensor of accounting software, the software does not work, and as a result the licensee cannot complete its books of account and therefore misses the opportunity to close an important business deal, the licensor could be liable for the value of that deal. This may be an exaggeration, but it illustrates the point. Consequential damages can include lost profits and the value of lost business or goodwill.

Consequential damages are unpredictable and potentially high—and can be particularly high in proportion to the value of the underlying deal. Therefore, it is customary for companies to agree, by contract, to exclude consequential damages. Thus, the following type of provision is very common:

"Consequential Damages Limitation/Fees Paid Limitation or Cap"

Limitation of Liability. NEITHER PARTY WILL BE LIABLE TO THE OTHER PARTY FOR ANY SPECIAL, CONSEQUENTIAL, EXEMPLARY OR INCIDENTAL DAMAGES (INCLUDING LOST OR ANTICIPATED REVENUES OR PROFITS RELATING TO THE SAME), ARISING FROM ANY CLAIM RELATING TO THIS AGREEMENT OR THE SUBJECT MATTER HEREOF, WHETHER SUCH CLAIM IS BASED ON WARRANTY, CONTRACT, TORT (INCLUDING NEGLIGENCE) OR OTHERWISE, EVEN IF AN AUTHORIZED REPRESENTATIVE OF SUCH PARTY IS ADVISED OF THE POSSIBILITY OF SUCH DAMAGES. THESE LIMITATIONS WILL APPLY NOTWITHSTANDING ANY FAILURE OF ESSENTIAL PURPOSE OF ANY LIMITED REMEDY. NEITHER PARTY'S AGGREGATE LIABILITY TO THE OTHER WITH RESPECT TO ANY AND ALL CLAIMS ARISING OUT OF OR RELATED TO THE SUBJECT MATTER OF THIS AGREEMENT WILL EXCEED THE AMOUNT OF LICENSE FEES PAYABLE BY LICENSEE HEREUNDER.

The first sentence disclaims all incidental and consequential damages. This leaves direct damages. The last sentence limits direct damages to a certain amount—the price of the deal.

By the way, if you were wondering why this provision is in capital letters, it is because limitations of liability are more likely to be enforceable if they are "conspicuous," and courts have recognized that capital letters make clauses conspicuous.

Why limit damages? Because the risk involved with high damages translates into a cost of doing business, and may make the cost of doing business higher than the benefit of the contract. Limiting damages also makes the potential gain from of litigating the agreement lower, and thus discourages lawsuits. In business-to-business arrangements, this is considered a valuable goal, even though it limits the parties' ability to enforce their contracts using the legal system. Note that the analysis is different for consumer agreements, where questions of public policy and unconscionability are more important than in a business context.

Warranty Disclaimers

Finally, we must understand warranty disclaimers—the other "capital letter" provisions. Warranties can arise, as exemplified above, by an express contractual provision. But they can also arise by implication. In business agreements, the most important implied warranties arise by statute under the Uniform Commercial Code. The Uniform Commercial Code is a set of uniform laws that covers commercial transactions. It is important that commercial laws be uniform so businesses in different states know what to expect from the law that governs their transactions. Each of the states in the United States has adopted the uniform commercial code, most with no modification.

Article II of the Uniform Commercial Code covers the sale of goods. Particularly in the case of over-the-counter software, courts have interpreted "goods" to include intellectual property and a "sale" to include a license of intellectual property. In addition, the line of demarcation between goods and services is sometimes difficult to draw in our new information economy. So to be cautious, lawyers must assume that the UCC, along with its implied warranties, applies to most transactions.

The UCC includes three warranties that arise by implication in every sale of goods: merchantability, fitness for a particular purpose, and title. In the case of hard goods like nuts and bolts, it is not difficult to understand what these warranties mean. If a bolt breaks apart the first time you tighten it, it is not merchantable. If you buy the bolt because the specifications book at the auto parts store says it will fit your car, and it does not, it is not fit for your particular purpose. If the bolt is still owned by the manufacturer and the store didn't own it to sell it to you, there was insufficient title to make the sale.

But what do these warranties mean for licenses of intellectual property? That is much more complex. If the software has a bug, is it still merchantable? If the software does not work on your computer, is it fit for your particular purpose? Title is a bit easier. The UCC specifically states that for intellectual property, the warranty of title includes a warranty of non-infringement. However, it is risky for licensors to make a broad warranty of non-infringement, as discussed further below.

The UCC does allow a licensor to disclaim implied warranties—in "conspicuous" provisions, of course—so we often see this kind of provision in a license agreement:

Warranty Disclaimer. EXCEPT FOR THE WARRANTIES EXPLICITLY SET FORTH IN THIS AGREEMENT, LICENSOR MAKES NO REPRESENTATIONS OR WARRANTIES OF ANY KIND, WHETHER ORAL OR WRITTEN, WHETHER EXPRESS, IMPLIED, OR ARISING BY STATUTE, CUSTOM, COURSE OF DEALING OR TRADE USAGE, WITH RESPECT TO THE SUBJECT MATTER HEREOF, IN CONNECTION WITH THIS AGREEMENT. LICENSOR SPECIFICALLY DISCLAIMS ANY AND ALL IMPLIED OR STATUTORY WARRANTIES OF TITLE, MERCHANTABILITY, FITNESS FOR A PARTICULAR PURPOSE, AND NON-INFRINGEMENT.

When an agreement includes a warranty disclaimer like this, "what you see is what you get." The only warranties that will apply are the express warranties in the agreement, not warranties implied by statute or common law. Of course, a court could ultimately decide that a disclaimer cannot be enforced, if the court finds it unconscionable or contrary to public policy. But most lawyers rely on the assumption that the UCC warranties can be disclaimed.

Advanced Topic—Intellectual Property Warranties

All of the above items can be applied to all types of contracts, but if you are going to analyze intellectual property licenses, you need to understand some additional points about intellectual property warranties. Remember the example warranty we used above? It looks straightforward on its face:

Non-Infringement Warranty. Licensor hereby represents and warrants to Licensee that the Software does not and will not infringe any third party's copyright, patent, trade secret, or trademark rights.

However, most intellectual property lawyers acting on behalf of the Licensor will object to this warranty. This is because not all intellectual property rights are alike: non-infringement warranties for copyrights and trade secrets are less risky than non-infringement warranties for patents and trademarks. Copyrights and trade secrets are "enabling" in the sense that reverse-engineering or independent development is a defense to infringement. For instance, if Author William in the United States writes a poem, and Arturo Guillermo in Italy writes the same poem independently, and both publish their poems, neither is infringing the other's copyright. Granted, it may be very unlikely that William and Guillermo will write the same poem independently, and one may sue the other anyway because he does not believe it possible. But if there is independent creation, there is no infringement. Similarly, if Listerine develops a formula for mouthwash that is a trade secret, and Colgate reverse-engineers the formula by chemical analysis but without access to Listerine's recipe, there is no trade secret misappropriation.

The story is different for patent rights. If Albert Einstein in Albuquerque develops a new pharmaceutical substance, then applies for a product patent on it, and Bertram Einstein in Boston, with no knowledge of Albert's patent application, later develops and sells the same substance, Bertram will infringe Albert's rights. It does not matter if Bertram sells his product first: as long as Albert invented the product first and filed a patent application, Bertram will be infringing. This problem is exacerbated by the fact that in the United States, patent applications are secret until issued. So, the following scenario is possible:

Date	Event
January 1, 2000	*A. Einstein invents the wonder drug Einsteinatin*
January 2, 2000	*B. Einstein invents the same wonder drug, and names it Wonderin, but does no patent it, preferring to keep the invention as a trade secret*
February 1, 2000	*B. Einstein begins selling Wonderin (having gotten FDA approval in record time)*
September 1, 2000	*A. Einstein files a product patent on Einsteinatin*
January 1, 2002	*B. Einstein's company goes public due to its record sales of Wonderin*
August 1, 2002	*A. Einstein's patent issues*
August 2, 2002	*A. Einstein sues B. Einstein and his company for patent infringement*

Bertram Einstein and his company are big trouble. What did they do wrong? They quickly commercialized a wonder drug. That's not normally considered wrong. They did not file a patent. That may have been an unfortunate choice, but it was by no means irrational; when the patent issues, everyone knows the secret formula for the drug, which may increase the likelihood of generics; patent protection is only 17 years, whereas trade secret protection can last forever. Could Bertram's company have done a patent search to find Albert's application? No, the application is secret. Could Bertram have found the patent on the day it issued and stopped selling Wonderin? Yes, if he is doing patent searches daily. But patent searches are expensive (using money better spent on developing wonder drugs), and moreover, patents only apply to a particular jurisdiction. Should Bertram and his company have known about Albert's invention? Possibly, but what if Albert is just a kook working in his basement who have never commercialized anything? Or what if Albert's basement, and his patent, is in Japan and Bertram Einstein is only doing business in the United States? In sum, Bertram Einstein and his company could be liable for a huge sum in patent infringement damages, without ever having stolen, copied, or misappropriated anything.

The same is true on a lesser scale with trademark applications, but for slightly different reasons. In some countries, the first to file a trademark gets the rights to it. In the United States, one gets rights in a trademark by using it, but the rights only extend to the geographic area in which it is used. If you have been using your mark in California for years, but unknown to you, another company is using the same mark in

Nome, Alaska, you may not be able to sell your product there—whether you have registered your mark or not. If you register your mark, the same Nome company can surface a year later and challenge it. The bottom line is that even if you use your mark and file registrations, you can never be sure that your mark is cleared, particularly in jurisdictions where you have not sold much, because independent "development" of the mark is not a defense.

The explanation is long, but the main point is this: A licensor cannot responsibly make a warranty that any product does not infringe patents or trademarks. On copyrights and trade secrets, a licensor can be reasonably sure that a product is non-infringing if the licensor has developed it in-house. For patents and trademarks, this is not the case.

For this reason, many licensors refuse to give unqualified patent or trademark warranties. However, there is a long divide between no warranty and an unqualified warranty, and several compromises are customary. Here are some of the qualified warranties that licensors typically propose:

"Best-of-Knowledge Warranty"

Intellectual Property Warranty. Licensor hereby represents and warrants to Licensee that the Software does not and will not infringe any third party's copyright or trade secret rights. Licensor hereby represents and warrants to Licensee that, to the best of Licensor's knowledge as of the Effective Date with no further investigation, the Software does not infringe any third party's patent or trademark rights.

This compromise limits the warranty to the best of Licensor's knowledge. Thus, the Licensor will not be liable for breach of warranty if the Licensor has no knowledge of a patent or trademark that the Software infringes. But this puts the Licensee in a difficult position: if a patent or trademark surfaces, there is no recourse under this warranty. Moreover, if the Licensor has indemnified the Licensee for any breach of warranty, and the Licensee gets sued for infringement, and the Licensee is left without an indemnity for this patent or trademark claim. This is sometimes addressed by broadening the indemnity to an intellectual property indemnity, rather than an indemnity for breach of warranty, for instance:

Intellectual Property Indemnity. Licensor shall defend or settle, and pay any damages finally awarded, claims, costs and fees (including reasonable attorneys' fees), with respect to any and all third party claims, demands, suits, actions, or proceedings brought against Licensee to the extent they arise from the allegation that the Software infringes any patent, copyright, trademark, trade secret, right of privacy or publicity, or any other intellectual property right of any third party.

As you can see, this gives the Licensee protection against third party claims while limiting the scope of the warranty to a manageable risk for the Licensor. What is the difference? If the Software infringes a patent, and the Licensor did not know about it, and the patent owner never files a claim against the Licensee, there is no breach of the agreement. Also, if the Licensee is sued, and the Licensor fulfills its indemnity obligations, similarly, there is no breach of the agreement. Contrast to the unqualified warranty, where once there is an infringement, the Licensor is in breach of the agreement.

There is another way of approaching this issue: limiting the remedies for breach of warranty. Recall for a moment the remedies for breach of warranty that are available absent any limitation. A breach of a warranty, like any breach of an agreement, can result in compensatory or direct damages, consequential damages, and possibly injunctive relief. In addition, contracts can usually be terminated for a material breach. However, this panoply of remedies means that a patent non-infringement warranty is terribly risky for a Licensor. Therefore, Licensors sometimes try to manage this risk by limiting the remedies for a breach of warranty. Thus:

Non-Infringement Warranty with "Sole Remedy" Limitation

Non-Infringement Warranty. Licensor hereby represents and warrants to Licensee that the Software does not and will not infringe any third party's copyright, patent, trade secret, or trademark rights.

Obligation to Defend Third Party Claims. Licensor shall defend, or at its option settle, all lawsuits, actions, claims, or demands ("Claims") against Licensee, and shall pay any associated third party damages, liabilities, judgments, and costs (including court costs) and fees (including attorneys' fees) arising therefrom, to the extent such Claims arise out of any breach of any warranty made by the Licensor pursuant to Section ___ (Warranty). The foregoing obligations of Licensor will be Licensee's sole remedy, and Licensor's sole obligation and liability, for breach of the warranty in Section ___ (Warranty).

If you cannot see the point of having a warranty with a remedy limited to an express obligation in the agreement, you are beginning to understand. A warranty with a limited remedy is like no warranty at all. There will be no action for breach of warranty, and arguably no termination of the agreement based on a breach of warranty.

A similar approach is common for performance warranties. Licensors argue, correctly, that software is never without bugs or problems. Thus, the argument goes, the performance warranties offered by a Licensor should have a limited remedy. For instance:

"Performance Warranty—Sole Remedy"

Performance Warranty Licensor warrants to Licensee that, for 90 days following the first delivery of the Software, the Software will perform in all material respects in accordance with its applicable published specifications. Licensee's sole remedy for breach of the foregoing warranty will be to have Licensor correct, within a reasonable period of time, any documented and reproducible defects in the Software that cause the Software not to perform in all material respects in accordance with its applicable published specifications.

Like the limited remedy for a breach of a non-infringement warranty, this means that a breach of the warranty is not a breach of the agreement, and the Licensee cannot terminate the agreement for breach, nor bring an action for damages, based on failure of the Software to perform correctly. Licensees object to this, and rightly so, because it means they will remain bound to the software license even if the software doesn't work. This usually precipitates a negotiation on the issue of whether a breach of a performance warranty should give the Licensee the right to rescind the agreement or get a refund of the license fee. (See the discussion of software revenue recognition in the chapter on royalties.)

Limitations of Liability, Redux

A third way to manage risk in indemnity provisions is to place liability caps on them. This is a blunt force approach, as compared to the fine strokes of limited remedies, narrower scope of claims, and defend/settle clauses. Here is an example:

Non-Infringement Warranty with Liability Limitation

Non-Infringement Warranty. Licensor hereby represents and warrants to Licensee that the Software does not and will not infringe any third party's copyright, patent, trade secret, or trademark rights.

Obligation to Defend Third Party Claims. Licensor shall defend, or at its option settle, all lawsuits, actions, claims, or demands ("Claims") against Licensee, and shall pay any associated third party damages, liabilities, judgments, and costs (including court costs) and fees (including attorneys' fees) arising therefrom, to the extent such Claims arise out of any breach of any warranty made by the Licensor pursuant to Section ___ (Warranties).

Limitation of Liability. LICENSOR'S AGGREGATE LIABILITY TO LICENSEE WITH RESPECT TO ANY AND ALL CLAIMS ARISING OUT OF OR RELATED TO THE SUBJECT MATTER OF THIS AGREEMENT WILL NOT EXCEED THE AMOUNT OF LICENSE FEES PAYABLE BY LICENSEE HEREUNDER.

The result is that while the Licensor has the obligation to defend, its liability for refusing to perform that obligation is limited to the amount of the license fee. Whether this is a meaningful limitation depends on the value of the deal. If the license fee is $10,000, the limitation is so effective that the indemnity is not a meaningful obligation. That amount of money will not even suffice to answer a complaint. If the license fee is $10 million, the limitation is not effective, because most suits will cost less. The usual compromise is somewhere in the middle.

Advanced Topic—More About Indemnities

The provisions used as examples above are simple versions of indemnities and the like. But you should recognize what more detailed indemnity provisions look like, and which details are customary. For instance, most indemnity provisions contain procedural limitations and remedies for the indemnitor. Here is a typical indemnity in a software license:

Intellectual Property Claims.

(a) Obligation to Defend. Licensor shall defend or settle, and pay any damages finally awarded, claims, costs and fees (including reasonable attorneys' fees), with respect to any and all third party claims, demands, suits, actions, or proceedings brought against Licensee to the extent they arise from the allegation that the Software infringes any United States patent issued as of the date of execution of this Agreement, copyright, trademark, trade secret, right of privacy or publicity, or any other intellectual property right of any third party.

(b) Procedures. The forgoing obligation of Licensor is subject to: (i) Licensee promptly notifying Licensor of any claim; (ii) Licensee allowing Licensor sole control of the defense; and (ii) Licensee cooperating with Licensor in such defense. Licensee may, but will not be obligated to, be represented by counsel of its choice and participate in the defense of the claim; provided, however, that the expense of such counsel and such participation will be borne by Licensee. Licensee shall not settle any such claim without the prior written consent of Licensor.

(c) Limitations. The foregoing obligations will not apply to the extent the infringement arises as a result of: (i) modifications to the Software made by any party other than Licensor; (ii) use of the Software outside the scope of the licenses granted herein; or (iii) combination of the Software with technology or products not supplied by Licensor.

Remedies. If the Software is held in any such suit to infringe and the use of Software is, or Licensor reasonably believes is likely to be, enjoined, Licensor shall have the option, as its own expense, to procure the right to continue using the Software, or replace same with non-infringing, functionally equivalent Software; or modify same to make them non-infringing; or refund the license fee for the Software.

Putting it all Together—Carve Outs and Limitations

This is where the rubber hits the road for licensing lawyers: can you analyze the allocation of risk provisions all together? If you do not analyze these provisions as a whole, you will fail your clients: You may end up negotiating points that are unimportant, or missing points that are important. Always keep in mind the decision you are helping your client to make: is doing this deal worth the risk? To answer this, you must analyze the value of the deal to your client, and the overall exposure of the contract's allocation of risk provisions.

First, it is worth nothing that there are at least two schools of thought about allocating liability in agreements. The first school of thought makes liability for one party as broad as possible, and minimizes liability for the other party, because the objective is to reduce the risk for the other party as much as possible. The second makes liability very narrow for each party, because low liability means there is less to be gained by suing for damages, and thus less motivation for either party to sue. In the spirit of full disclosure, I favor the latter approach. (Is this a conflict of interest? It favors the reputation of the transactional lawyer by making clients less likely to litigate their agreements. In my defense, I have observed that most clients dislike litigation as much as their attorneys do.) However, some lawyers, and many companies, strongly favor the former. This often seems to be the case, perhaps not surprisingly, for large companies with plenty of resources to enforce their agreements in court. However, these companies are deep pockets, too, and thus targets for litigation, so the calculus is not simple.

To read all the allocation of risk provisions together, you must understand carve-outs. For instance, the following is extremely common:

> **Limitation of Liability.** EXCEPT FOR LIABILITY ARISING OUT OF SECTION ___ (NON-DISCLOSURE), NEITHER PARTY WILL BE LIABLE TO THE OTHER PARTY FOR ANY SPECIAL, CONSEQUENTIAL, EXEMPLARY OR INCIDENTAL DAMAGES (INCLUDING LOST OR ANTICIPATED REVENUES OR PROFITS RELATING TO THE SAME) ARISING FROM ANY CLAIM RELATING TO THIS AGREEMENT OR THE SUBJECT MATTER HEREOF. EXCEPT FOR LIABILITY ARISING OUT OF SECTION ___ (INDEMNITY), NEITHER PARTY'S AGGREGATE LIABILITY TO THE OTHER WITH RESPECT TO ANY AND ALL CLAIMS ARISING OUT OF OR RELATED TO THE SUBJECT MATTER OF THIS AGREEMENT WILL EXCEED THE AMOUNT OF LICENSE FEES PAYABLE BY LICENSEE HEREUNDER.

The first carve-out is common because consequential damages are the type of damages that tend to arise from breach of confidentiality obligations. The second carve-out is common because the fees payable under most agreements are small enough so that a cap on liability for the indemnity obligation makes the obligation meaningless. To correctly assess the allocation of risk in a contract, you need to understand all the carve-outs.

Here is a quick checklist of provisions you should review before you begin your analysis:

Issue	Checklist Item	Comments
Limitation of Liability	Is there a monetary cap?	A cap on liability dictates how much concern you will have about exposure for monetary damages in the remaining provisions.
	Are consequential damages disclaimed?	A common exception is the non-disclosure provision
	Are there any carve-outs or exceptions to the cap?	A common exception is the indemnity provision
Warranties	Are they vague and therefore easy to breach?	Be particularly aware of warranties about "high standards" "quality" and "moral character"
	Is there a limited remedy?	Common remedies for performance warranties: repair or replace (or refund) Common remedies for IP warranties: indemnity for third party claims

	Are the facts underlying the warranty within your client's control?	See discussion of patent, trademark claims
Indemnities	What claims are covered?	Is this a general indemnity? An intellectual property indemnity? An indemnity for breach of warranty?
	Are the facts that would underlie a covered claim within your client's control?	See discussion of patent and trademark indemnities
	Is this an obligation to indemnify, or just defend?	
	Does the cap on liability, if any, apply?	

Once you have ascertained all of the above about your agreement, you should be able to locate the allocation of risk scheme on the chart below. Go through each of the rows of this chart, make sure you understand the analysis for each example, and then you will be ready to do battle with the best!

Warranty*	Indemnity	Limitation of Liability	Comments
• Intellectual Property	• General	• Fees Paid • Consequentials • Carve Out for Indemnity	• Licensor is indemnifying for all liability, including breach of warranty. • Patent/Trademark non-infringement warranties are risky. (See Best-of-Knowledge warranty) • High exposure, particularly for patent infringement. • Limitation of Liability may not be meaningful because there is no limitation for the indemnity, which covers all breaches of the agreement.
• Intellectual Property	• General	• Fees Paid • Consequentials	• Licensor is indemnifying for all liability, including breach of warranty. • Low exposure. Limitation of liability to fees paid will probably make the indemnity ineffectual. • Patent/Trademark non-infringement warranties are risky. Here, although the liability will be low, the Licensee may terminate the agreement based on the breach.
• Intellectual Property	• Indemnity for Breach of Warranty	• Fees Paid • Consequentials • Carve Out for Indemnity	• Licensor is indemnifying for breach of warranty. • High exposure, particularly for patent infringement. • Patent/Trademark non-infringement warranties are risky.
• Intellectual Property	• Indemnity for Breach of Warranty	• Fees Paid • Consequentials	• Licensor is indemnifying for breach of warranty. • Low exposure. Limitation of liability to fees paid will probably make the indemnity ineffectual. • Patent/Trademark non-infringement warranties are risky. Here, although the liability will be low, the Licensee may terminate the agreement based on the breach.
• Intellectual Property	• Defend and Settle	• Fees Paid • Consequentials • Carve Out for Indemnity	• Licensor is defending third party claims for breach of warranty. • High exposure, particularly for patent infringement.
• Intellectual Property	• Defend and Settle	• Fees Paid • Consequentials	• Licensor is defending third party claims for breach of warranty. • Low exposure. Limitation of liability to fees paid will probably make the indemnity ineffectual.
• Intellectual Property—Best of Knowledge	• General	• Fees Paid • Consequentials • Carve Out for Indemnity	• Licensor is indemnifying for all liability, including breach of warranty. • High exposure, particularly for patent infringement. • Limitation of Liability may not be meaningful because there is no limitation for the indemnity, which covers all breaches of the agreement.
• Intellectual Property—Best of Knowledge	• General	• Fees Paid • Consequentials	• Licensor is indemnifying for all liability, including breach of warranty. • Low exposure. Limitation of liability to fees paid will probably make the indemnity ineffectual.
• Intellectual Property—Best	• Indemnity for Breach of	• Fees Paid • Consequentials	• Licensor is indemnifying for breach of warranty. Note that for a best of knowledge warranty, this will not cover all infringements, only those the

Warranty*	Indemnity	Limitation of Liability	Comments
of Knowledge	Warranty	• Carve Out for Indemnity	Licensor does not know about. • Low exposure for patent/trademark claims because of best of knowledge qualifier.
• Intellectual Property—Best of Knowledge	• Indemnity for Breach of Warranty	• Fees Paid • Consequentials	• Licensor is indemnifying for breach of warranty. Note that for a best of knowledge warranty, this will not cover all infringements, only those the Licensor does not know about. • Low exposure. Limitation of liability to fees paid will probably make the indemnity ineffectual.
• Intellectual Property—Best of Knowledge	• Defend and Settle	• Fees Paid • Consequentials • Carve Out for Indemnity	• Licensor is defending third party claims for breach of warranty. Note that for a best of knowledge warranty, this will not cover all infringements, only those the Licensor does not know about. • High exposure, particularly for patent infringement.
• Intellectual Property—Best of Knowledge	• Defend and Settle	• Fees Paid • Consequentials	• Licensor is defending third party claims for breach of warranty. Note that for a best of knowledge warranty, this will not cover all infringements, only those the Licensor does not know about. • Low exposure. Limitation of liability to fees paid will probably make the indemnity ineffectual.
• Performance	• General	• Fees Paid • Consequentials • Carve Out for Indemnity	• Licensor is indemnifying for all liability, including breach of warranty. • High exposure, particularly for patent infringement. • Limitation of Liability may not be meaningful because there is no limitation for the indemnity, which covers all breaches of the agreement.
• Performance	• General	• Fees Paid • Consequentials	• Licensor is indemnifying for all liability, including breach of warranty. • Low exposure. Limitation of liability to fees paid will probably make the indemnity ineffectual.
• Performance	• Indemnity for Breach of Warranty	• Fees Paid • Consequentials • Carve Out for Indemnity	• Licensor is indemnifying for breach of warranty. • Main exposure is for claims by Licensee's customers.
• Performance	• Indemnity for Breach of Warranty	• Fees Paid • Consequentials	• Licensor is indemnifying for breach of warranty. • Main exposure is for claims by Licensee's customers. Limitation of liability to fees paid will probably reduce this somewhat.
• Performance	• Defend and Settle	• Fees Paid • Consequentials • Carve Out for Indemnity	• Licensor is defending third party claims for breach of warranty. • Main exposure is for claims by Licensee's customers.
• Performance	• Defend and Settle	• Fees Paid • Consequentials	• Licensor is defending third party claims for breach of warranty. • Main exposure is for claims by Licensee's customers. Limitation of liability to fees paid will probably reduce this somewhat.
• Performance —Sole remedy	• N/A	• N/A	• Low Risk.

*Note: Chart presumes there is a disclaimer of implied warranties.

NOTES

XIII: Week 12: Ethics and Negotiation

This chapter outlines some of the ethical principals in the drafting and negotiation of transactional agreements. It focuses on two subjects: the rules of professional responsibility that you must follow by law, and the "rules" of custom and practice that are considered professional courtesy in the transactional practice. It also contains some tips and exercises for negotiating license agreements.

Professional Rules

The professional ethics rules can be difficult to apply to this practice, because most of them were developed in litigation contexts. This is a brief summary of some of the rules of professional ethics that apply to transactional practice.

- **Conflicts of Interest** Rule 3-310 (Citations here are to the Rules of Professional Conduct of the State Bar of California.) states that a member of the bar "shall not accept ... representation of a client without providing written disclosure to the client where ... the member has a legal, business, financial, professional, or personal relationship with a party or witness in the same matter." Thus, if you or your firm previously represented Thumbelina in a litigation matter, and Fair Share asked you to represent it in connection with the value added reseller deal mentioned in the hypotheticals, you would need to seek a waiver by Thumbelina to agree to the representation.

- **Communications with Represented Parties**. Rule 2-100 states that a member of the bar may not communicate about the subject matter of the representation with a party the member knows to be represented by another lawyer, unless the member has the consent of the other lawyer. Thus, suppose you represent Fair Share in negotiating the value added reseller agreement, and Thumbelina is conducting negotiations through Kaiser Sose, its Director of Business Development, along with outside counsel. Sose calls you to discuss the agreement. You must decline to discuss the subject matter of the value added reseller agreement unless you have Thumbelina's attorney's permission to talk directly to Sose.

- **Client Confidentiality**. Remember that your client's confidential information is to be used by you only to further your client's interests. So for instance, if your client is a company whose stock is traded on a public market, and you are representing it in a major co-marketing deal whose announcement is likely to increase your client's stock price, you may not give a "stock tip" to a friend, or buy the stock yourself, to garner a gain. Such behavior would violate the rules of ethics, and possibly make you the subject of criminal prosecution for violating federal securities laws.

How to Conduct a Negotiation

This may seem incredibly basic, but here is how a negotiation usually works.

- Thumbelina and Fair Share want to do a deal. The parties or their attorneys write a "deal memo," "memorandum of understanding," "letter of intent," or "term sheet" describing the basic business points. For a license, this should include, at a minimum, the exclusivity, scope, territory, royalties, and duration of the license.
- An attorney for Thumbelina draws up an initial draft of the agreement based on the term sheet. The party who drafts the document "has the pen" or "controls the document." After reviewing it with Thumbelina, the attorney (or Thumbelina) sends it to Fair Share.
- Now, the iterative process of negotiation and revision begins. This consists of Fair Share's attorneys making revisions to the document and sending it back to Thumbelina, or convening a negotiation to discuss open issues.
- These days, drafts are often passed back and forth by e-mail. Alternatively, one side may do a handwritten markup of the document for the other side to review and make revisions accordingly.
- When the parties have agreed on all the terms, and all the information in the contract is complete, each side signs the agreement. These days, faxed signatures are often exchanged, with signed copies following by post. Each side usually signs two copies, and each retains one fully executed copy.

The Unwritten Rules of Custom and Professional Courtesy

It is one thing to obey the law, another to act properly in a professional setting. The following is a list of things you might consider when you begin to participate in negotiations as an attorney. Although none of these things are required by law, they may help you enjoy your practice more, and avoid burning too many bridges by making mistakes in the unwritten etiquette of practice.

- When you revise an agreement, always send a "redline" or marked copy. If you cannot produce one for technical or logistical reasons, you should explain why.

• When you revise a contract based on a negotiation, make all the revisions you have stated you will make. If for some reason you do not, explain why. This will give you credibility, which is essential to a smooth negotiation.

• It is customary for one side to raise all of the issues it intends to raise based on a particular draft at once. If you cannot do this, you should state that your comments or drafts are "subject to your client's review" or that you may need to raise further issues about a particular subject. If you do not do this, your opponent will complain that you have taken a "second bite at the apple." This is a concept that comes from litigation, where parties who fail to raise issues can lose their opportunity to raise them. In negotiations, of course, any party can raise an issue at any time and refuse to sign until it is resolved. But this will infuriate your opponents.

• When you conduct a telephone conference or meeting, introduce everyone first, and state whether or not each person is an attorney. You would be surprised how seldom this happens. By the way, it can seem rude to ask "Jane, are you an attorney?" One way to finesse this is to say, "Jane, I just want to check, are you outside counsel or in-house at the company?" If Jane is not an attorney, you will find out, and if she is, she will not be offended.

• Leave items to be discussed in brackets, or indicate that the issue is open in another clear fashion. This will help avoid overlooking open points.

Negotiation Tips

The day will come when you are called upon to negotiate on your client's behalf. To some, this comes naturally. If you are one of those lucky few, consider yourself blessed. For the rest of us, negotiation can be frightening and stressful, especially at first. Here are some tips to help you. Once you have negotiated a bit, it will get easier and less stressful. In the end, many attorneys find negotiation the most gratifying part of their career—but this may seem amazing when you first set out to do it.

- **Focus on Interests, Not Positions** This is the basic rule of negotiation, and there are plenty of good books outlining this philosophy.[viii] Positions do not get you to a resolution. Explaining your client's needs will help you come to creative solutions.
- **Knowledge is Power**. The best antidote for nervousness is to prepare. Read the document you are negotiating carefully; you should know it the most closely of anyone in the negotiation. Know your client and your client's objectives. Know your opponent; look up your opponent's qualifications on his

or her company's or law firm's web page, or on Martindale Hubbell (whose search engine is available at http:// www.martindale.com/locator/home.html) If your opponent is not a specialist in intellectual property licensing, you may legitimately need to explain some concepts.

- **Be Polite**. Negotiation is not a personal attack, it is a discussion. Do not take it personally. Every lawyer lets negotiations get under his skin, sometimes. But try to distance yourself from feeling insecure; that distance will help you think clearly. Your opponent is not your enemy. Over the years, I have received many referrals of client business from opposing counsel. Make your opponents respect you, not hate you.

- **Win Points, Not Games** The lawyer who wins a point in a negotiation is not necessarily the smartest or most aggressive lawyer. Humiliating your opponent may be tempting, but it is not usually effective. If you perceive your opponent as weak, be careful! Weak negotiators are defensive and often unreasonable. Educate your opponent, instead of shaming him.

- **When in Doubt, Be Quiet**. Silence is extremely effective. When you are unprepared or stuck for an answer, just be silent. You will be amazed what happens. I learned this once when I got laryngitis—and my negotiating improved.

- **Help Your Opponent Agree with You**. Your opponent may need to sell a deal point to a client, to a board of directors, or to himself. Give him the ammunition to do this, and you have given him a reason to agree with you.

- **Don't Put Up with Bullies**. Contrary to myth, most lawyers are fairly nice people to deal with in professional settings. But someday, I assure you, you will run into a lawyer who is aggressive, neurotic, belligerent, rude, or downright psychotic. Do not let yourself be drawn in. Treat lawyers who have tantrums the way you would treat a child. If someone is screaming at you, the proper response is, "I am going to hang up the phone now. Why don't you call me back when you've calmed down?" Chances are, this break will not delay matters a bit, as your negotiation is probably getting nowhere.

As an exercise in class, we will negotiate the following indemnity provisions. First, assume that the Licensor has proposed its provision. The Licensee should take 5-10 minutes to review the provision and make a list of issues. Then, the Licensee should explain his or her concerns and issues, and ask for changes or concessions.

Next, assume that the Licensee has proposed its provision. Reverse the roles, and give the Licensor a chance to ask for changes.

Indemnity Proposed by Licensor

Indemnification. Licensor shall defend or settle, and pay any damages finally awarded, court costs and fees (including reasonable attorneys' fees), with respect to any and all third party claims, demands, suits, actions, or proceedings brought against Licensee (collectively, "Claims") to the extent they arise the allegation that the Software infringes any U.S. patent issued as of the date of execution of this Agreement, copyright, trademark, trade secret, or right of privacy or publicity of any third party, provided that Licensee promptly notifies Licensor of any Claim, and Licensee allows Licensor sole control of the defense of such Claim. Licensee shall have the right, but not the obligation, to be represented by counsel of its choice and to participate in the defense of the claim; provided, however, that the expense of such counsel and such participation shall be borne by Licensee; and provided, further, that the Licensee shall not settle any such claim without the prior written consent of Licensor. If the Software is held in any such suit to infringe and the use of Software is, or Licensor reasonably believes is likely to be, enjoined, Licensor shall have the option, as its own expense, to procure the right to continue using the Software, or replace same with non-infringing, functionally equivalent Software; or modify same to make them non-infringing; or refund the pro-rated value of the Software over a lifetime of five (5) years, and accept the return of the Software.

Indemnity Proposed by Licensee

Indemnification. Licensor shall defend, indemnify and hold harmless Licensee against any claims, losses, expenses, damages, costs and fees (including without limitation attorneys' fees) of Licensee (collectively, "Claims") that arise from the allegation that the Software infringes any patent, copyright, trademark, trade secret, right of privacy or publicity, or other intellectual property right of any third party. Licensee shall promptly notify Licensor of any Claim. Licensee shall have the right, but not the obligation, to be represented by counsel of its choice and to participate in the defense of the claim. If the Software is held in any such suit to infringe and the use of Software is, or Licensor reasonably believes is likely to be, enjoined, Licensor shall, as its own expense, procure the right to continue using the Software, or replace same with non-infringing, functionally equivalent Software; or modify same to make it non-infringing; or refund the license and maintenance fees paid by Licensee for the Software, and accept the return of same.

NOTES

XIV: Week 13: Substantive Review: Miscellaneous Contract Law

This chapter discusses some of the "boilerplate" provisions that usually appear at the end of an agreement in the "general" or "miscellaneous" section. Many of these provisions are uncontroversial and do not generate much negotiation. Nevertheless, it is very important to read and understand these provisions in every contract you review.

Choice of Law and Venue – Forum Shopping and Expense of Litigation.

We all remember from law school that when one party brings suit against another, the plaintiff can select where the suit will be brought, subject to the constitutional and subject matter limits of jurisdiction. (*See International Shoe Co. v. Washington,* 326 U.S. 310 (1945).) Thus, plaintiffs' attorneys often spend a great deal of effort selecting the jurisdiction and venue that will be most amenable to success on their claim. This is called "forum shopping." Many corporations worry that there will be legitimate venue for claims against them in all 50 states, because they do business nationwide or have offices in most states. In addition, a corporation that promulgates many form agreements that are almost identical (such as an end user license or a services agreement used with the corporation's customers) prefers to have all the agreements governed by the same state law, so that if a court issues a decision on a particular contract term, the corporation can take action to manage its risks on all the contracts.

In order to avoid forum shopping and make the task of interpreting agreements more certain, most written contracts designate a particular state's law to govern interpretation, and set a site, usually within a particular state or county, to designate the forum in which disputes will be resolved. At the time of contract execution, of course, neither side knows for certain which claims will arise. So while the parties can make some guesses as to which jurisdiction and venue will be best to resolve claims they are likely to make, the forum assessment task is much more difficult. For this reason, most forum selections in contracts are based on cost. To litigate a dispute in a state other than its own, a corporation must usually hire local counsel and pay travel expenses for its principals. Thus, most corporations wish to select the jurisdiction and venue of their home state.

For instance, a company with headquarters in California will often include a provision such as:

> **Governing Law and Venue.** This Agreement will be construed in accordance with the laws of the State of California that applies to contracts made, entered into and performed solely in California

and solely by and between California residents, without regard to its conflict of laws principles. Any dispute arising out of this Agreement will be subject to the exclusive jurisdiction of the state and federal courts located in Santa Clara County, California, and the parties hereby waive any objection to such jurisdiction and venue.

There are a few points worth noting about this language. The first is merely a point of drafting, but it is better to write "Any dispute arising out of this Agreement will be subject to the exclusive jurisdiction of the state and federal courts located in Santa Clara County, California" than "Any dispute arising out of this Agreement must be resolved in the state and federal courts located in Santa Clara County, California." The latter seems to say that all disputes must go to court, and this is not the point. The point, instead, is that neither party may unilaterally select another jurisdiction. Second, be careful to write "the state and federal courts located in Santa Clara County, California" rather than "the courts of Santa Clara County, California." Read literally, the latter means state or municipal courts only. This could cause problems for disputes that are exclusively matters of federal law or that are better resolved in federal court.

Generally, courts will enforce a jurisdiction and venue selection in a contract. But there are exceptions. Most of the pitfalls that can arise on these provisions arise because of the process of bargaining during the contract negotiation. Because the location of dispute resolution is a "binary" issue—in other words, if the parties come from different states, only one party can win—the provisions can be difficult to negotiate. The most frequent compromises are the "your backyard" concept, and the process of picking a midpoint.

The "your backyard" concept acts to discourage each party from bringing suit, and requires that each party must sue in the other party's home state:

> **Governing Law and Venue.** This Agreement will be construed in accordance with the laws of the State of California that applies to contracts made, entered into and performed solely in California and solely by and between California residents, without regard to its conflict of laws principles. Any dispute arising out of this Agreement, if brought by Licensor, will be subject to the exclusive jurisdiction of the state and federal courts located in Santa Clara County, California. Any dispute arising out of this Agreement, if brought by Licensee, will be subject to the exclusive jurisdiction of the state and federal courts located in New York, New York. The parties hereby waive any objection to such jurisdiction and venue.

Note that the governing law designation does not change depending on the site of jurisdiction and venue. This is so that if there is a question about interpretation the contract, prior to the time when it would be clear who would bring suit, an attorney does not have to perform two analyses under different state laws to answer the question. Generally, this works because a state's courts will be willing and able to apply another state's laws.

The midpoint idea is simply to choose a geographical midpoint for dispute resolution. Thus, for the same Licensor and Licensee in California and New York:

> **Governing Law and Venue.** This Agreement will be construed in accordance with the laws of the State of California that applies to contracts made, entered into and performed solely in California and solely by and between California residents, without regard to its conflict of laws principles. Any dispute arising out of this Agreement, if brought by Licensor, will be subject to the exclusive jurisdiction of the state and federal courts located in Chicago, Illinois, and the parties hereby waive any objection to such jurisdiction and venue.

Note two points about this approach. First, governing law remains that of one of the parties. The parties could instead designate the law of Illinois, but there is no particular reason to do so. The substance of Illinois law is not "midway" between that of New York and California. Second, the courts of Illinois will not exercise jurisdiction if they cannot do so under the limits of jurisdiction under the United States constitution. The parties in a contract cannot agree to give the court jurisdiction where there would be none as a matter of law.

The next section discusses arbitration. The issues that arise from the constitutional limits of jurisdiction do not apply to arbitrators, because arbitrators resolve disputes by private arrangement, and as private persons, are not subject to the limits the constitution places on government courts. Thus, the parties above could have selected arbitration in Chicago, and there would be little question that this could be effectuated. Most states have adopted the Uniform Arbitration Act, which provides that contracts involving interstate commerce and providing for arbitration is enforceable. (Under *Southland Corp. v. Keating*, 104 S. Ct. 852 (1984), a state cannot require judicial resolution of claims that by contract must be arbitrated.)

You may be surprised that the decision-making process described above is not based on substantive law, but on considerations like geographic proximity and costs. This is because, for most intellectual property contracts, the lion's share of substantive law issues may be controlled by federal intellectual property law or by state contract law that conforms with the Uniform Commercial Code. While there are some particular quirks of state law that may arise, and these can be a useful basis for forum shopping, the differences tend to be minimal, and marginal enough to make them unpredictable at the time of execution of the agreement, before any disputes have arisen.

The same is not true for international agreements. The selection of the law of one country rather than the other can be critical. See the chapter on International Issues for a more detailed discussion.

Alternative Dispute Resolution

The miscellaneous provisions of your contract also may designate the form of dispute resolution procedure to be applied to disputes related to the contract. If you do not designate any dispute resolution method, each party may bring a contract dispute to court. However, you may wish to designate another form of dispute resolution to use before, or instead of, a lawsuit. The types of dispute resolution procedures used in intellectual property licenses are usually escalation, mediation, and binding or non-binding arbitration[ix].

Escalation is a procedure for resolving disputes within the management structure of the parties to the agreement. Here is an example of an escalation provision:

> **Escalation**. If the parties are unable to resolve any dispute between themselves, either party may, upon written notice to the other, submit such dispute to the parties' chief executive officers, who shall meet to attempt to resolve the dispute by good faith negotiations. In the event the parties are unable to resolve such dispute within 30 days after such notice is received, either party may proceed with any other dispute resolution procedure available under this Agreement.

Escalation provisions can be very effective to avoid lawsuits. If the provision requires a senior management member to be involved, the parties are unlikely to allow disputes to go unresolved, because there may be very negative consequences within the corporate organization to a manager who must require a senior executive to solve his or her problems. The busier the senior executive, the more effective the provision.

Mediation provisions require a neutral, outside third party to attempt to help the parties resolve their dispute. A mediator does not have the authority to make a binding decision, but due to the mediator's training in dispute resolution, may be able to help both sides resolve their differences amicably by providing a disinterested viewpoint.

Arbitration is a more formal procedure that involves the presentation of evidence and rendering of a decision by one or more arbitrators. Arbitration can be non-binding (in which case it may seem more like mediation) or binding. Binding arbitration cannot be "appealed" to a court—it is a final decision.

> **Arbitration**. Any dispute, controversy or claim arising under this Agreement will be settled by binding arbitration under the rules of the American Arbitration. The parties shall select an arbitration panel of three arbitrators, as follows. Each party shall appoint one arbitrator. The two arbitrators so appointed will appoint a third arbitrator. The parties will be entitled to discovery to the extent permitted by the Federal Rules of Civil Procedure of the United States. This Section ___ will not be construed to prevent either party from applying to a court of competent jurisdiction for injunctive relief. One half of costs of the arbitration will be borne by each party. Each party will bear its own expenses related to the arbitration, including attorneys' fees.

There is much literature about the pros and cons of arbitration, and this book will not seek to present the question in detail. The process of deciding *ex ante* whether arbitration will favor your client is difficult. However, there is some conventional wisdom about when arbitration is preferable. First, most litigators will tell you that arbitration usually shorter, but is not necessarily cheaper, than a lawsuit. Second, they will warn you that the unavailability of appeal for binding arbitration is dangerous, and the availability of re-litigating a non-binding arbitration makes it a needless expense. (In fact, arbitration awards can be appealed, but the standard for overturning them is high. See *Barnes v. Avery*, 16 S.E.2d 861 (1941); Section 12 of the Uniform Arbitration Act.) However, arbitration can avoid the publicity of a lawsuit (which is good or bad depending on whether your client wishes to use publicity as a weapon).

Also, conventional wisdom says that arbitrators tend to "split the baby"—in other words, they may try to come to a middle-of-the-road decision even when neither side is served by such a decision. Thus, conventional wisdom dictates that intellectual property disputes are not well handled by arbitration, because intellectual property is a property right and usually gives rise to injunctive relief, and therefore, intellectual property disputes should usually be resolved entirely in one party's favor.

Large corporations with active litigation staff usually develop policies about dispute resolution. If you are working for such a client, it is probably best to defer to the client's policies. For smaller clients with less dispute experience, you should look to the literature on alternative dispute resolution to help your client make a decision. The American Arbitration Association referenced in the provision above is only one of the local organizations that facilitate alternative dispute resolution. You client may prefer another organization.

As described above in the section on International Issues, arbitration may be particularly desirable for international agreements. Also, if you do use a binding arbitration provision, be sure to specify a site for arbitration. If you do not, there may be no useful forum in which to resolve the site of arbitration, as courts may refuse to exercise jurisdiction over the dispute.

Assignment

Of all the provisions in the miscellaneous section of an agreement, the assignment provision is usually the most controversial. This is because it bears upon the ability of the parties to avoid breach or termination on the agreement when they engage in corporate transactions such as mergers, acquisitions, public offerings, and reorganizations.

Corporate transactions usually involve either an asset purchase or a stock purchase. In the case of an asset purchase, the issue of assignability of contracts is clearer. If, for instance, a television network wishes to sell off its Web site to another corporation, it might sell (i.e. assign) the intellectual property involved in the Web site, transfer the employees who worked in relevant areas, sell any real estate it owned in connection with the business, and most important, transfer any agreements (content licenses, leases, advertising agreements, co-marketing agreements, etc.) that related to the business. Because all the assets go to a new entity, it is clear that the agreements need to be assigned. When lawyers work on such transactions, one task is to determine whether all of these agreements can be assigned. This process is part of what is called "due diligence" for the transaction. If a critical contract cannot be assigned (for instance, the contract under which the Web site gets all its news or graphics) the transaction may founder.

Most stock purchase transactions involve, in effect, the purchase of a large block of the stock of one corporation (the "target") by another (the "acquiror"). Usually, the buyer purchases either a controlling interest or all of the target's stock. Due diligence for mergers is more complex than for asset purchases, because, at the outset, it is not clear whether the transaction will constitute an assignment to a different entity. A common form of merger is called the "reverse triangular merger," which effectively preserves the target as a separate going concern.[x] Yet, some courts have found that such a transaction constitutes an "assignment by operation of law." To see why this is important, take a look at some of the sample assignment provisions below.

Contract Language	Interpretation
Target may assign in connection with merger, acquisition, reorganization or sale of all or substantially all of its assets *relating to this Agreement*.	Assignment is allowed. (*Cyrix Corp. v. Intel Corp.*, 803 F. Supp. 1200 (E.D. Tex 1992)) But if the underlined language is missing, spin transactions or sales of divisions that do not constitute substantially all of the target's assets are not allowed.
This Agreement will be binding upon and will inure to the benefit of the parties and their respective successors and assigns.	This language, absent a separate restriction on assignment, suggests the agreement is assignable. *Adams v. Howard* (CCNY) 22 F. 656; *Dunkley Co. v. California Packing Corp.* (2d Cir. N.Y.) 277 F. 996 (1921).
Neither this Agreement nor any rights under this Agreement may be assigned by Target, voluntarily or by operation of law, without the prior written consent of Licensor.	Not assignable.
Neither this Agreement nor any rights under this Agreement may be assigned by Target, without the prior written consent of Licensor.	Where assignment by operation of law is not expressly prohibited, case law is divided.
Neither this Agreement nor any rights under this Agreement may be assigned by Target without the prior written consent of Licensor, *which consent will not be unreasonably withheld*.	The underlined language is not thought to be restrictive enough to give comfort to an acquiror.

Other Provisions

Here are some brief descriptions of other provisions you may find in the miscellaneous section of an agreement.

Notices

This provision describes how notices that are required by the contract must be sent. The objective in these provisions is generally to avoid the "mailbox rule" and to clarify who in an organization should receive notices.

The main points to review in a notice provision have to do with the practicality of receiving notice. If your deal is between a United States corporation and a corporation in a country with slow or limited mail delivery, you may wish to allow for longer notice periods to take into account postal delays, or you may wish to require the use of a private carrier such as FedEx or DHL. Also, be careful about allowing notice under new forms of communication technology that are not appropriate. For instance, you may not want to allow fax notice, particularly without a written confirmation. Faxes tend to get lost or mis-transmitted. E-mail notice might also not be appropriate (except in Web-based deals where electronic communication is the core of the transaction). Registered letters, which are the traditional form of notice, get plenty of attention in most offices. The very convenience and ubiquity of fax and email may be the reason to require a registered post notice— because it will not be likely to be ignored or forgotten.

Here is an example of a notice provision:

Notices. Any notice required or permitted under the terms of this Agreement or required by law must be in writing and must be: (a) delivered in person; (b) sent by first class registered mail, or air mail, as appropriate; or (c) sent by overnight air courier, in each case properly posted and fully prepaid to the appropriate address set forth in the preamble to this Agreement. Either party may change its address for notice by notice to the other party given in accordance with this Section. Notices will be considered to have been given at the time of actual delivery in person, three business days after deposit in the mail as set forth above, or one day after delivery to an overnight air courier service.

Waiver

Parties performing a contract can lose their right to seek redress for breach of the contract if they "sit on their rights" too long. So, for instance, suppose a software end user license provides that the licensee must use the software only at a specific location (sometimes called a "site license"). But one year after the beginning of the license, the licensee informs the licensor in a letter that it has relocated its headquarters to a new address. Communications both ways flow to and from that address, including the licensee's regular license fee payments. Two years after the license has commenced, licensor sues for breach of the site restriction. A court may refuse to give licensor redress, because licensor was aware of the new site and accepted payments based on that knowledge. This would be based on an equitable principle known as "laches" or "waiver."

Parties attempt to contract out of these equitable limitations on remedies in a provision like this:

Waiver. Any waiver of the provisions of this Agreement or of a party's rights or remedies under this Agreement must be in writing to be effective. Failure, neglect, or delay by a party to enforce the provisions of this Agreement or its rights or remedies at any time, will not be construed as a waiver of such party's rights under this Agreement and will not in any way affect the validity of the whole or any part of this Agreement or prejudice such party's right to take subsequent action. No exercise or enforcement by either party of any right or remedy under this Agreement will preclude the enforcement by such party of any other right or remedy under this Agreement or that such party is entitled by law to enforce.

Integration or "Entire Agreement"

This section memorializes the default "parol evidence rule"—that the written contract "integrates" all of the negotiations up until the time of contract execution. Thus, the executed contract takes precedence over any oral discussions or any prior term sheets, letters of intent, or correspondence relating to the deal. This section also usually requires amendments to be in writing.

Integration. This Agreement (including the Exhibits) contains the entire agreement of the parties with respect to the subject matter of this Agreement and supersedes all previous communications, rep re sentations, understandings and agreements, either oral or written, between the parties with respect to said subject matter. No terms, provisions or conditions of any purchase order, acknowledgment or other busi ness form that either party may use in connection with the transactions contemplated by this Agreement will have any effect on the rights, duties or obligations of the parties under, or otherwise modify, this Agreement, regardless of any failure of a receiving party to object to such terms, provisions or conditions. This Agreement may not be amended, except by a writing signed by both parties

Severability

A severability provision is used to avoid the unenforceablity of one provision voiding the entire contract.

Severability. If any term, condition, or provision in this Agreement is found to be invalid, unlawful or unenforceable to any extent, the parties shall endeavor in good faith to agree to such amend ments that will preserve, as far as possible, the intentions expressed in this Agreement. If the parties fail to agree on such an amendment, such invalid term, condition or provision will be severed from the remaining terms, conditions and provisions, which will continue to be valid and enforceable to the fullest extent permitted by law.

This type of provision is especially important if you are writing a consumer contract, or a contract includes non-competition provisions, or other provisions that your are concerned may be perceived as violating public policy and as such adjudged unenforceable.

NOTES

XV: Hypotheticals

To assist you in using this book and having discussions in class, I have created some hypothetical deals described below. None of these are intended to represent actual companies. In particular, none are intended to be any of my clients.

"Joint Development Agreement"—Guesstimate and Berkeley Fixed-Gear Messenger Collective. Guesstimate is a business that collects information about traffic in major metropolitan areas and makes it available to subscribers of its service through a web-based application. This means that the subscriber can simply sign on to the service using an ordinary browser program, put in a password, and receive detailed information about traffic, including estimates of the traffic delay time in traveling between specific points. Guesstimate's technology was developed by high-school student while working part time for UC Berkeley in the computer sciences department. Berkeley Fixed-Gear Messenger Collective is a non-profit organization that serves as a trade support group for bicycle messengers—particularly those who ride fixed-gear bicycles (i.e. that do not coast). BFGMC offers services to its members such as package delivery referrals, health insurance, and discounted bicycle gear. Through its operations, BFGMC has developed a referral system that selects and routes messengers efficiently. But this system is a paper system, not an automated one. Due to a recent generous grant to purchase computer equipment, BFGMC now wants to automate its referral system. BFGMC and Guesstimate want to enter into an agreement to jointly develop the automated system.

"Volume Purchase Agreement"—ZipSwitch, Inc. and MegaRouter Corporation. ZipSwitch is a fab-less semiconductor company that designs and sells chips (manufactured by a third party fabricator) that perform switching of data. ZipSwitch's unique design for its "Interlock Switches" was inspired by the technology in an ordinary household zipper. The chips use software developed by ZipSwitch that can only be used on ZipSwitch's products. ZipSwitch has been in business for three years and is on the verge of filing its S-1 to initiate a public offering. MegaRouter is ZipSwitch's biggest customer, a multi-billion dollar company that designs, manufactures and sells specialized routers for the telecommunication industry. It purchases ZipSwitch's products and uses them as a component in its routers. In their proposed transaction, MegaRouter will purchase its requirements of interlock switches from ZipSwitch. In return, ZipSwitch will offer MegaRouter attractive terms and prices.

"Co-Branded Web Service"—Hairs2U and General Petroleum Unlikely bedfellows in the on-line space, General Petroleum is an oil company and Hairs2U provides a service that allows its users to do a "virtual makeover" by trying different hairstyles and hair colors on a photograph provided by the user. Hairs2U does not just paste a hair photo on top of yours, it analyzes the growth patterns of your hair based on your photo, and uses sophisticated computer graphics to make the virtual hairstyle look the way it will on you. It offers this service to the public at its web site at Hairs2U. These days, the latest craze in shampoo additives is called "heavy oil"—derived from crude oil that has been infused with salt and certain minerals, which is easy to obtain from oceanic oil spills. General Petroleum has created oil spill collection technology that produces heavy oil, and has just made a public offering for its partly-owned subsidiary Heavy-2-O, Inc. which sells a line of hair care products containing Heavy Oil. Heavy-2-O wants Hairs2U to create a version of the Hairs2U service that is sponsored by Heavy-2-O, and has the "look and feel" of the existing Heavy-2-O web site.

"VAR/Systems Integrator"—Thumbelina Software and Fair Share Office Systems Fair Share Office Systems is a business with a modest mission—to help minority- and woman- owned businesses set up state of the art local area computer networks to run their businesses. Fair Share provides technology from soup to nuts, including PC hardware, network servers and telecommunications systems, integrated voice mail, and other technology. To do this, Fair Share has entered into contracts with many suppliers of all these kinds of technology. One of them is Thumbelina systems, which provides software that can scan a heat-sensitive pad for the thumbprint for the user. Thumbelina provides the heat-sensitive pads, which are relatively easy to manufacture. But its "secret sauce" is the software that analyzes and verifies the thumbprint. Thumbelina allows value-added resellers like Fair Share to sell licenses to its software and distribute its heat-sensitive pad units.

XVI: Appendix—Sample Exam Questions

The following are some sample exams that I have used in prior courses:

Final Exam—Intellectual Property Licensing, Fall 1999

```
Subject: Term Sheet For Development Deal
Author: Heather Meeker, Technology Transactions, WSGR
Date: 12/21/99
```

Below is an email from Carl, who wants a quick turnaround on his development and marketing agreement. I don't have a model handy for this agreement, but you can use the agreements I showed you in the past few months.

```
FORWARD>>>_____
Subject: Term Sheet For Development Deal
Author: Carl Coder, VP of Business Development, KillerApp Software
Date: 12/21/99
```

Heather:

Hi, I know we haven't spoken in a while. We have recently changed our company name from AppCo to KillerApp Software. Our application software product, which we sell for Windows, Apple and Linux platforms, lets our customers quickly delete files that are outdated and taking up space, using a special algorithm to find files that are likely to be junk files. We need to develop an interface that helps run our application on files located on all types of disk drives. The interface needs to be ultra-fast, so we can't use any commercially available ones.

The attached term sheet is for our partnering deal with ZoomDisk Inc. Can you write a simple, short agreement for this? I would prefer an agreement we could also use as a model again on the next deal, which will probably be with another disk drive company. We want to get these deals done quickly, so please don't go overboard with the legalese.

This is a really big deal for us. Could you try and get this to me soon i.e. tomorrow so that we can sign this prior to our press release at the trade show?

Carl.

Statement of Work

- The interface will be written in C++ and will interface between the KillerApp software product and the device driver for ZoomDisk's ULTRA MEGA storage devices. The interface will be developed by KillerApp and ZoomDisk's technical engineers, working together.

- When the interface is developed, KillerApp and ZoomDisk will work together to market the interface to their customers. Each company will be able to distribute and sell the product, bundled with its own product. We will make joint sales calls, cooperate at trade shows, and do joint press releases. Each company will pay a royalty of 5% of net sales.

- In addition, if either KillerApp or ZoomDisk makes a sale of its own product to a customer because of a joint sales call or referral, the company making the sale will pay a 5% commission to the other company.

Due Date	Milestones/Deliverables	Responsible Party
1/5/00	Delivery of API for ZoomDisk's ULTRA MEGA drives	ZoomDisk
1/5/00	Delivery of 5 sample ULTRA MEGA drives	ZoomDisk
1/15/00	Delivery of KillerApp software and API to ZoomDisk	KillerApp
2/15/00	Final Specification for Interface	Both
3/15/00	Completion of Interface for Windows version of KillerApp Product	Both
3/15/00	Completion of Interface for Linux version of KillerApp Product	Both
3/15/00	Completion of Interface for Apple version of KillerApp Product	Both
4/1/00	Alpha test	KillerApp
5/1/00	Beta test	Both
6/1/00	Product Release	

Final Exam—Intellectual Property Licensing, Fall 2000

Your client, HairWizard, Inc., provides a service that allows its users to do a "virtual makeover" by trying different hairstyles and hair color on a photograph provided by the user. HairWizard does not just paste a hair photo on top of yours, it analyzes the growth patterns of your hair based on your photo, and uses sophisticated computer graphics to make the virtual hairstyle look the way it will on you. It offers this service to the public at its web site at HairWizard. The service is free of charge, but HairWizard needs to find some creative ways of generating revenue.

Your client, HairWizard, sends you the following email message:

-----Original Message-----

From: Hill, Samuel

Date: Friday, December 24, 2000 7:30 p.m.

To: Meeker, Heather

URGENT -- Need Agreement!

Hi Heather,

I am sending you the term sheet for our private label partnership with General Petroleum. We need an agreement right away! Could you please send me a draft by tomorrow? If you have questions, call me on my cell phone.

I will be at Heavenly Ski Lodge.

Sam

Private Label E-Commerce Partnership Term Sheet

• These days, the latest craze in shampoo additives is called "heavy oil" -- derived from crude oil that has been infused with salt and certain minerals, which is easy to obtain from oceanic oil spills. General Petroleum has created oil spill collection technology that produces heavy oil, and developed a line of hair care products containing Heavy Oil. It wants to launch these products over the Web using the brand "Heavy-2-O."

• General Petroleum is spinning out a new subsidiary called Heavy-2-O, Inc. to do this deal.

• The launch date for the site is 1/1/01.

• This is a 3 year deal.

• The site we are putting together for this deal will allow a visitor to read about Heavy-2-O's products and order products on line. HairWizard will contribute its proprietary makeover system (including the software and the images needed to run it) to the web site, but Heavy-2-O's designers will give the site the look and feel of Heavy-2-O's existing site, and Heavy-2-O will be operating the site once it's launched.

• Heavy-2-O's existing site describes the products developed by Heavy-2-O, but does not yet allow visitors to order on line. Heavy-2-O will have its e-commerce on line by the launch date. We want to make sure the e-commerce system is up and running by March 1 at the latest, or we want to get out of the deal, because we expect most of the money to come from product sales.

• This is an exclusive deal. We want to be the only makeover system on the Heavy-2-O web site. We will not promote any products other than Heavy-2-O's products on our site. However, if our revenue is less than $500,000 in the first year, we want to be able to convert the deal to a non-exclusive deal.

• We will place a link on our home page at www.HairWizard to the new site.

• Here is the revenue sharing for the deal: We get 50% of all ad revenues and 5% of sales of products on pages of the web site that contain our makeover system.

• We are concerned about the speed and quality of the Heavy-2-O site. General Petroleum is a big company, but it doesn't have much experience with Web design. We want the site to meet a set of service levels for speed, number of hits, and criteria for e-commerce fulfillment. Our technical gurus can provide you with this information before we sign the agreement, but I don't have it now.

• We want to make sure Heavy-2-O always uses the latest version of our makeover system on the new site.

XVII: Appendix—Form Agreements

The following form agreements were developed by me and my students in connection with the seminar at Hastings. Two of the agreements are model papers for the final examination given in the class. The exam hypotheticals are also included here for your reference.

NOTES

XVIII: Form 1: "Shrink Wrap" Type End User License

End User License Agreement

This End User License Agreement (the "Agreement") is a legal agreement between you (either an individual or an entity) and Company regarding the use of Company's software entitled _____, version ___, which may include user documentation provided in "online" or electronic form (the "Software"). By [opening the sealed Software packages and/or by using the Software] [filling in the user information and clicking the button marked "I Accept" below], you agree to be bound by the terms of this Agreement. If you do not agree to the terms of this agreement, promptly return the unopened disk package and accompanying items (including printed materials and binders or other containers) to the place you obtained them for a full refund.[xi]

Grant of License. This Agreement permits you to use[xii] one copy of the specified version of the Software, for internal purposes only, on only one computer, and only by one user, at a time.[xiii] If you have purchased multiple licenses for the Software, then at any time you may have as many copies of the Software in use as you have licenses. The Software is "in use" on a computer when it is loaded into the temporary memory[xiv] (i.e. RAM) or installed into the permanent memory (e.g., hard disk, CD-ROM, or other storage device) of that computer.

Copyright. The Software is owned by Company or its suppliers or licensors and is protected by United States copyright laws and international treaty provisions. Therefore, you may not use, copy, or distribute[xv] the Software without authorization. You may (a) make one copy of the Software solely for backup or archival purposes[xvi], or (b) transfer the Software to a single hard disk provided you keep the original solely for backup or archival purposes. You may not copy the printed materials accompanying the Software, nor print copies of any user documentation provided in "online" or electronic form.

Restrictions. You may not rent, lease, or loan[xvii] the Software, but you may transfer your rights[xviii] under this Agreement permanently, provided you transfer this Agreement, the Software and all accompanying printed materials, retain no copies, and the recipient agrees to the terms of this Agreement. You may not reverse engineer, decompile, or disassemble the Software,[xix] except to the extent the foregoing restriction is expressly prohibited by applicable law. You may not modify, or create derivative works[xx] based upon the Software.

Limited Warranty. Company warrants that the media on which the Software is furnished under normal use will be free from defects in materials and workmanship[xxi] for a period of ninety (90) days from the date of receipt. This warranty is valid only for the original purchaser. Some states do not allow limitations on implied warranties, so the above limitation may not apply to you. Company's entire liability and your exclusive remedy[xxii] under this warranty will be replacement of the defective media that does not meet Company's limited warranty and that is returned to Company or an Company authorized representative with a copy of your receipt. This limited warranty is void if failure of the Software has resulted from accident, abuse, or misapplication. Any replacement Software will be warranted for the remainder of the original warranty period or thirty (30) days, whichever is longer.

THIS WARRANTY GIVES YOU SPECIFIC LEGAL RIGHTS. YOU MAY HAVE OTHERS WHICH VARY FROM STATE TO STATE.[xxiii]

NO OTHER WARRANTIES. YOU ASSUME ALL RESPONSIBILITIES FOR SELECTION OF THE SOFTWARE TO ACHIEVE YOUR INTENDED RESULTS, AND FOR THE INSTALLATION OF, USE OF, AND RESULTS OBTAINED FROM THE SOFTWARE. TO THE MAXIMUM EXTENT PERMITTED BY APPLICABLE LAW, COMPANY DISCLAIMS ALL OTHER WARRANTIES, EITHER EXPRESS OR IMPLIED, INCLUDING BUT NOT LIMITED TO IMPLIED WARRANTIES OF MERCHANTABILITY, FITNESS FOR A PARTICULAR PURPOSE,[xxiv] AND NONINFRINGEMENT WITH RESPECT TO THE SOFTWARE AND THE ACCOMPANYING WRITTEN MATERIALS. SOME STATES DO NOT ALLOW LIMITATIONS ON IMPLIED WARRANTIES, SO THE ABOVE LIMITATION MAY NOT APPLY TO YOU.[xxv]

NO LIABILITY FOR CONSEQUENTIAL DAMAGES. YOU ASSUME THE ENTIRE COST OF ANY DAMAGE RESULTING FROM THE INFORMATION CONTAINED IN OR COMPILED BY THE SOFTWARE. TO THE MAXIMUM EXTENT PERMITTED BY APPLICABLE LAW, IN NO EVENT WILL COMPANY OR ITS SUPPLIERS OR LICENSORS BE LIABLE FOR ANY DAMAGES WHATSOEVER (INCLUDING, WITHOUT LIMITATION, DAMAGES FOR LOSS OF BUSINESS PROFITS, BUSINESS INTERRUPTION, LOSS OF BUSINESS INFORMATION, OR OTHER PECUNIARY LOSS) ARISING OUT OF THE USE OR INABILITY TO USE THE SOFTWARE, EVEN IF SUCH PARTY HAS BEEN ADVISED OF THE POSSIBILITY OF SUCH DAMAGES.[xxvi] IN NO EVENT WILL COMPANY'S TOTAL LIABILITY TO YOU FOR ALL DAMAGES IN ANY ONE OR MORE CAUSE OF ACTION EXCEED THE AMOUNT PAID BY YOU FOR THE SOFTWARE. THIS LIMITATION WILL APPLY REGARDLESS OF THE FAILURE OF THE ESSENTIAL PURPOSE OF ANY LIMITED REMEDY.[xxvii] BECAUSE SOME STATES DO NOT ALLOW THE EXCLUSION OR LIMITATION OF LIABILITY FOR CONSEQUENTIAL OR INCIDENTAL DAMAGES, THE ABOVE LIMITATION MAY NOT APPLY TO YOU.[xxviii]

U.S. Government-Restricted Rights. The Software and accompanying documentation are deemed to be "commercial computer Software" and "commercial computer Software documentation," respectively, pursuant to DFAR Section 227.7202 and FAR Section 12.212,[xxix] as applicable. Any use, modification, reproduction release, performance, display or disclosure of the Software and accompanying documentation by the U.S. Government will be governed solely by the terms of this Agreement and will be prohibited except to the extent expressly permitted by the terms of this Agreement.

Export Restrictions. You may not download, export, or re-export the Software (a) into, or to a national or resident of, any country to which the United States has embargoed goods, or (b) to anyone on the United States Treasury Department's list of Specially Designated Nationals or the U.S. Commerce Department's Table of Deny Orders.[xxx] By downloading or using the Software, you are representing and warranting that you are not located in, under the control of, or a national or resident of any such country or on any such list.

General. This Agreement is governed by the laws of the United States and the State of California, without reference to conflict of laws principles. Any dispute between you and Company regarding this Agreement will be subject to the exclusive venue of the state and federal courts in the state of California.[xxxi] This Agreement is the entire agreement between you and Company and supersedes any other communications or advertising with respect to the Software an documentation. If any provision of this Agreement is held invalid, the remainder of this Agreement will continue in full force and effect.

Should you have any questions concerning this Agreement, or if you desire to contact Company for any reason, please contact:

_____

NOTES

XIX: Form 2: "OEM" Software Distribution Agreement

SOFTWARE SOURCE CODE OEM LICENSE AGREEMENT

This Software Source Code OEM License Agreement ("**Agreement**") is entered into as of _____ ("**Effective Date**") by and between _____, with offices at _____ ("**Licensor**") and **[OEM]**, a _____ corporation with offices at _____ ("**OEM**").

WHEREAS Licensor has developed certain Software (as defined below); and

WHEREAS OEM and Licensor wish the users of OEM's products to be able to use such software.

NOW, THEREFORE, the parties agree as follows:

1. Definitions

1.1 "**Software**" means the Licensor software described in **Exhibit A**, all Modifications, and any Updates supplied by Licensor under this Agreement.

1.2 "**OEM Products**" means any OEM products described in **Exhibit A**.

1.3 "**Modification**" means a modification, revision, enhancement, or other derivative work of the Software created by OEM under Section 2.1(a).

1.4 "**Bundled Product**" means a OEM Product that is combined with one copy of the Software, in object code or executable form only.

1.5 "**Update**" means any correction, update, upgrade, patch or other modification or addition to the Software.

1.6 "**Affiliate**" of a party means any entity that controls, is controlled by, or is under common control with that party, where "control" means ownership or control, direct or indirect, of more than 50% of the stock or other equity interest entitled to vote for the election of directors or equivalent governing body.

2. License Grants

2.1 **License.** Subject to the terms and conditions of this Agreement, Licensor hereby grants to OEM a royalty-free, nonexclusive, worldwide, nontransferable, nonsublicenseable license during the term of this Agreement:

(a) to create Modifications of the Software, solely to make the Software compatible with the OEM Products, and to create a reasonable number of copies of the source code of the Software as necessary to create such derivative works;

(b) to combine copies of the Software, in object code form only, with OEM Products to create Bundled Products;

(c) to distribute copies of the Software, in object code form only, only as part of Bundled Products;

(d) to use the Software solely to provide technical support for the Bundled Products;

(e) to reproduce copies of the Software, in object code form only, solely as necessary to exercise the rights granted in clauses (b), (c), and (d);

(f) subject to the terms and conditions of the end user license set forth in **Exhibit B**, a royalty-free, nonexclusive, worldwide, nontransferable, nonsublicenseable license right to use copies of the Software, up to the number of internal use copies specified in **Exhibit A**, solely for OEM's own internal business purposes, and not on behalf of any third party or otherwise on a "service bureau" basis.

2.2 **End User Licensing.** OEM shall distribute each copy of the Software with an end user license agreement substantially in the form attached hereto as **Exhibit B**.

2.3 **Proprietary Notices.** On each Software copy, OEM shall reproduce all copyright or other proprietary notices contained in or on the Software, as provided by Licensor.

2.4 **Distribution**. OEM may distribute copies of the Software directly to end users, or by selling such copies to third party resellers (collectively "**Distributors**") for resale to other Distributors or end users. Except for the right to use Distributors in accordance with this Section 2.4, OEM may not sublicense any of the rights or licenses granted under Section 2.1 to any third party.

2.5 **Delivery of Software**. On the Effective Date, Licensor shall deliver to OEM one copy of the Software, in source code format.

2.6 **Ownership**. Licensor will retain all right, title, and interest in the Software, and all intellectual property rights therein. OEM shall not remove, modify, or obscure any copyright or other proprietary notices on the Software. Licensor hereby reserves all rights not expressly granted to OEM in this Agreement. OEM hereby assigns and shall assign to Licensor all Modifications and any copyrights, or other intellectual property rights (except rights in OEM's trademarks) relating thereto. OEM shall, as may be requested by Licensor to effect and perfect the assignments and transfers contained herein, take any action and execute any documents reasonably requested by Licensor.

2.7 **Bundling Obligation**. During the term of this Agreement, OEM shall distribute the OEM Product only in connection with the Bundled Product and only in accordance with the branding obligations in Section 3.1.

3. Use of Licensor Trademarks

3.1 **Co-Branding. [Add any terms regarding OEM's rights or obligations to place Licensor's brand on OEM's product]**.

3.2 **Authorized Uses**. OEM may state that the Bundled Product includes the Software, and may use in its packaging, marketing, promotional and advertising materials of the Bundled Products such applicable trademarks, trade names and logos of Licensor (collectively, the '**Licensor Trademarks**') in connection therewith, but only as set forth, and in the manner indicated, on Exhibit D. Before any such use, OEM must provide to Licensor samples of any such materials, and OEM shall not engage in any use of any Licensor Trademark not approved by Licensor. If Licensor does not object within 5 business days after receipt of such samples, the materials will be deemed approved. Licensor shall not unreasonably withhold or delay its approval of such materials.

3.3 **Ownership by Licensor**. Any and all goodwill arising from OEM's use of the Licensor Trademarks will inure solely to the benefit of Licensor. OEM shall not assert any claim to the Licensor Trademarks (or any confusingly similar mark) or such goodwill. OEM shall execute such documents as Licensor may request from time to time to record or effectuate Licensor's ownership of the Licensor Trademarks and related goodwill. OEM shall not register any Licensor Trademark, or any mark confusingly similar to any Licensor Trademark, in any jurisdiction.

4. **Fees**. In consideration of the co-branding and bundling obligations of OEM under this Agreement, Licensor shall pay to OEM the fees specified in **Exhibit A**.

5. **Training, Support and Maintenance**. Licensor's obligations regarding training, Updates, support and maintenance for the Software; the respective rights and responsibilities of Licensor and OEM for such training, support and maintenance; and any charges to OEM for such training, support or maintenance; are set forth in **Exhibit C**.

6. Term and Termination

6.1 **Term**. This Agreement will commence on the Effective Date and continue for an initial term of one year unless earlier terminated as set forth herein. Thereafter, this Agreement will renew for additional one year terms unless and until either party provides written notice to the other party, at least 30 days prior to the expiration of the then-current term, of its intention not to renew this Agreement.

6.2 **Default**. If either party defaults in the performance of any of its material obligations hereunder and if any such default is not corrected within 30 days after notice in writing, by the other party, then the other party, at its option, may, in addition to any other remedies it may have, thereupon terminate this Agreement by giving written notice of termination to such party.

6.3 **Insolvency**. This Agreement may be terminated by either party, upon written notice, (i) upon the institution by the other party of insolvency, receivership or bankruptcy proceedings or any other proceedings for the settlement of its debts, (ii) upon the institution of such proceedings against the other party, which are not dismissed or otherwise resolved in its favor within 60 days thereafter, (iii) upon the other party's making a general assignment for the benefit of creditors, or (iv) upon the other party's dissolution or ceasing to conduct business in the ordinary course.

6.4 Survival.

(a) The parties' rights and obligations of Sections 2.3, 2.6, 3.3, 4, 6.4, 7, 8.3, 9, 10 and 11 will survive any termination or expiration of this Agreement.

(b) Upon expiration or termination of this Agreement, all of OEM's rights and licenses with respect to the Software will terminate, except (i) OEM's may continue to use one copy of the Software, in accordance with this Agreement, to support and maintain copies of the Bundled Product properly distributed under this Agreement; (ii) each Software end user license properly graded before the effective date of termination will survive in accordance with its terms; and (iii) unless this Agreement is terminated by Licensor pursuant to Section 6.2 or 6.3, OEM may dispose of copies of the Software incorporated into Bundled Products on the effective date of termination, in accordance with OEM's royalty and other obligations under this Agreement.

7. Infringement Indemnity

7.1 **Indemnity.** Licensor, at its expense, shall defend any third party claim brought against OEM to the extent based on a claim that the Software, in the form delivered by Licensor to OEM, when used as provided for by this Agreement, infringes any copyright or trade secret of any third party. Licensor shall pay any award against OEM, or settlement entered into on OEM's behalf, based on such infringement, but only if OEM notifies Licensor promptly in writing of the claim, provides reasonable assistance in connection with the defense and settlement thereof, and permits Licensor to control the defense and settlement thereof. Licensor will have no liability to the extent the alleged infringement is caused by any modification or combination of the Software with the OEM Product or other non-Licensor equipment, programs or data, where the Software alone would not have given rise to the claim.

7.2 **Licensor Options.** In the event of an infringement action against OEM with respect to the Software, or in the event Licensor believes such a claim is likely, Licensor may, at its option (i) appropriately modify the Software licensed hereunder, or substitute other non-infringing Software, so long as such modification or substitution does not materially alter the functionality of the Software; (ii) obtain a license with respect to the applicable third party intellectual property rights; or (iii) if neither (i) nor (ii) is commercially practicable, terminate this Agreement and OEM's licenses hereunder. If use of any Software copy is enjoined, Licensor shall refund to OEM the royalty paid to Licensor with respect thereto, depreciated on a 5-year straight-line basis from the date of initial distribution of such copy by OEM.

7.3 **Entire Liability.** The obligations of this Section 7 set forth Licensor's entire liability for actual or alleged infringement of intellectual property rights.

8. Warranty and Disclaimer

8.1 **Warranty.** Licensor warrants that, for a period of _____ ("**Warranty Period**"), the Software will conform to the documentation therefor. Licensor's sole liability, and OEM's sole remedy, with respect to such warranty will be Licensor's obligation to correct errors with a level of effort commensurate with the severity of the error. Licensor warrants that the copy of the Software delivered to OEM under Section 2.5 will not contain any virus, Trojan horse, worm, or other software routines or hardware components designed to permit unauthorized access, to disable, erase, or otherwise harm software, hardware or data ("**Virus**"). OEM's sole remedy with respect to breach of such warranty will be Licensor's obligation to deliver a new copy of the Software without such Virus.

8.2 **Exclusions.** The warranty under Section 8.1 will not extend to problems that result from: (i) OEM's failure to implement all Updates to the Software issued to OEM by Licensor; (ii) any alterations of or additions to the Software performed by parties other than Licensor; (iii) misuse of the Software; or (iv) use of the Software in conjunction with products not supplied or approved by Licensor.

8.3 **DISCLAIMER.** EXCEPT AS SET FORTH IN SECTION 8.1, LICENSOR MAKES NO WARRANTY, EXPRESS, IMPLIED, STATUTORY, OR OTHERWISE, AND SPECIFICALLY DISCLAIMS ANY WARRANTY OF MERCHANTABILITY OR FITNESS FOR A PARTICULAR PURPOSE, WITH RESPECT TO THE SOFTWARE.

9. LIMITATION OF LIABILITY. LICENSOR'S LIABILITY ARISING OUT OF THIS AGREEMENT WILL NOT EXCEED THE AMOUNTS RECEIVED BY LICENSOR FROM OEM HEREUNDER. LICENSOR WILL NOT BE LIABLE FOR LOST PROFITS OR ANY CONSEQUENTIAL, SPECIAL, INCIDENTAL, OR INDIRECT DAMAGES, HOWEVER CAUSED AND ON ANY THEORY OF LIABILITY, ARISING OUT OF THIS AGREEMENT. OEM ACKNOWLEDGES THAT FEES AGREED UPON BY LICENSOR AND OEM ARE BASED IN PART UPON THESE LIMITATIONS, AND THAT THESE LIMITATIONS WILL APPLY NOTWITHSTANDING ANY FAILURE OF ESSENTIAL PURPOSE OF ANY LIMITED REMEDY.

10. Confidentiality

10.1 **Confidential Information**. The term "**Confidential Information**" means any information disclosed by one party to the other pursuant to this Agreement that is in written, graphic, machine readable or other tangible form and is marked "Confidential," "Proprietary" or in some other manner to indicate its confidential nature. Confidential Information may also include oral information disclosed by one party to the other pursuant to this Agreement, provided that such information is designated as confidential at the time of disclosure and is reduced to writing by the disclosing party within a reasonable time (not to exceed 30 days) after its oral disclosure, and such writing is marked in a manner to indicate its confidential nature and delivered to the receiving party.

10.2 **Confidentiality**. Each party shall treat as confidential all Confidential Information of the other party, shall not use such Confidential Information except to exercise its rights and perform its obligations under this Agreement herein, and shall not disclose such Confidential Information to any third party. Without limiting the foregoing, each of the parties shall use at least the same degree of care it uses to prevent the disclosure of its own confidential information of like importance, to prevent the disclosure of Confidential Information of the other party. Each party shall promptly notify the other party of any actual or suspected misuse or unauthorized disclosure of the other party's Confidential Information.

10.3 **Exceptions**. Confidential Information excludes information that: (i) was in the public domain at the time it was disclosed or has become in the public domain through no fault of the receiving party; (ii) was known to the receiving party, without restriction, at the time of disclosure, as demonstrated by files in existence at the time of disclosure; (iii) is disclosed with the prior written approval of the disclosing party; (iv) was independently developed by the receiving party without any use of the Confidential Information; (v) becomes known to the receiving party, without restriction, from a source other than the disclosing party, without breach of this Agreement, by the receiving party; or (vi) is disclosed generally to third parties by the disclosing party without restrictions similar to those contained in this Agreement. The receiving party may disclose the other party's Confidential Information to the extent such disclosure is required by order or requirement of a court, administrative agency, or other governmental body, but only if the receiving party provides prompt notice thereof to the disclosing party to enable the disclosing party to seek a protective order or otherwise prevent or restrict such disclosure.

10.4 **Confidentiality of Agreement**. The parties shall cooperate in issuing jointly approved press releases concerning this Agreement, including without limitation an initial such release within 30 days after the Effective Date. After such press releases, each party may disclose the existence of this Agreement, but agrees that the terms and conditions of this Agreement will be treated as Confidential Information; provided, however, that each party may disclose the terms and conditions of this Agreement: (i) as required by any court or other governmental body; (ii) as otherwise required by law; (iii) to legal counsel of the parties; (iv) in confidence, to accountants, banks, and financing sources and their advisors; (v) in connection with the enforcement of this Agreement or rights under this Agreement; or (vi) in confidence, in connection with an actual or proposed merger, acquisition, or similar transaction.

10.5 **Source Code Security**. OEM shall use the Software only under carefully controlled conditions for the purposes set forth in this Agreement, and shall inform all employees who are given access to the Software by OEM that the source code of the Software is a confidential trade secret of Licensor. OEM shall restrict access to the source code of Software to those employees of OEM who have agreed to be bound by a confidentiality obligation substantially in the form of this Section 10, and who have a need to access the source code to carry out the purposes of this Agreement. Upon request by Licensor, OEM shall provide Licensor with the names of all individuals who have accessed such materials, and shall take all actions reasonably required to recover any such materials in the event of loss or misappropriation, or to otherwise prevent their unauthorized disclosure or use. OEM shall indemnify and hold harmless Licensor for any breach of such confidentiality obligation or of this Agreement by any of OEM's employees, agents and representatives.

11. General

11.1 **Governing Law**. This Agreement will be governed by and interpreted in accordance with the laws of the State of California, U.S.A., without reference to its conflict of laws principles.

11.2 **Forum Selection**. All disputes arising out of this Agreement are subject to the exclusive jurisdiction of the state and federal courts located in Santa Clara County, California, and the parties hereby submit to the personal jurisdiction and venue of these courts.

11.3 **Indemnification of Licensor**. Except for intellectual property infringement claims covered by Section 7, OEM shall indemnify and hold Licensor harmless against any liability, or any litigation cost or expense (including attorneys' fees), arising out of third party claims against Licensor as a result of OEM's use or distribution of the Software.

11.4 **Partial Invalidity**. If any provision in this Agreement is found invalid or unenforceable, then the meaning of such provision will be construed, to the extent feasible, so as to render the provision enforceable, and if no feasible interpretation would save such provision, it will be severed from the remainder of this Agreement, which will remain in full force and effect, and the parties shall negotiate, in good faith, a substitute, valid and enforceable provision that most nearly effects the parties' intent in entering into this Agreement.

11.5 **Independent Contractors**. The parties are independent contractors. Nothing contained herein will constitute either party the agent of the other party, or constitute the parties as partners or joint venturers. OEM shall make no representations or warranties on behalf of Licensor with respect to the Software.

11.6 **Modification**. No alteration, amendment, waiver, cancellation or any other change in any term or condition of this Agreement will be valid or binding on either party unless the same is mutually agreed to in writing by both parties.

11.7 **Waiver**. The failure of either party to enforce at any time any of the provisions of this Agreement, or the failure to require at any time performance by the other party of any of the provisions of this Agreement, will not be construed to be a waiver of such provisions, or in any way affect the right of either party to enforce such provision thereafter. The express waiver by either party of any provision of this Agreement will not constitute a waiver of any future obligation to comply with such provision.

11.8 **Assignment**. This Agreement will be binding upon and inure to the benefit of the parties hereto and their respective successors and assigns; provided, however, that neither party shall assign any of its rights, obligations, or privileges (by operation of law or otherwise) hereunder without the prior written consent of the other party. Notwithstanding the foregoing, however, (i) either party may assign this Agreement to a successor in interest (or its equivalent) of all or substantially all of its relevant assets, whether by sale, merger, or otherwise; and (ii) Licensor (and any assignee of Licensor) may assign this Agreement to any of its Affiliates. Any attempted assignment in violation of this section will be void.

11.9 **Notices**. Any notice required or permitted to be given by either party under this Agreement will be in writing and personally delivered or sent by commercial courier service (e.g., DHL), or by first class airmail (certified or registered if available), to the other party at its address first set forth above, or such new address as may from time to time be supplied hereunder by the parties hereto. If mailed, notices will be deemed effective 5 working days after deposit, postage prepaid, in the mail.

11.10 **Export Regulations**. OEM acknowledges that the Software is subject to United States export controls, pursuant to the U.S. Export Administration Regulations. OEM shall comply with all applicable provisions of the Export Administration Regulations, and shall not export, reexport, transfer, divert or disclose, directly or indirectly, including via remote access, the Software, any confidential information contained or embodied in the Software, or any direct product thereof, except as authorized under the Export Administration Regulations.

11.11 **Force Majeure**. Notwithstanding anything else in this Agreement, and except for the obligation to pay money, no default, delay or failure to perform on the part of either party will be considered a breach of this Agreement if such default, delay or failure to perform is shown to be due to causes beyond reasonable control of the party charged with a default, including, but not limited to, causes such as strikes, lockouts or other labor disputes, riots, civil disturbances, actions or inactions of governmental authorities or suppliers, epidemics, war, embargoes, severe weather, fire, earthquakes, acts of God or the public enemy, nuclear disasters, or default of a common carrier.

11.12 **Entire Agreement**. The terms and conditions of this Agreement, including all Exhibits hereto, constitute the entire agreement between the parties and supersede all previous agreements and understandings, whether oral or written, between the parties hereto with respect to the subject matter hereof.

IN WITNESS WHEREOF, the parties hereto have caused this Agreement to be signed by duly authorized officers or representatives as of the date first above written.

Licensor	OEM
By: _____	By: _____
Print Name: _____	Print Name: _____
Title: _____	Title: _____

EXHIBIT A
Software, OEM Products, and Fees

Software: [describe software]

OEM Product: [describe OEM product]

Fees: (e.g. per copy distributed, or one-time fee)

Internal Use Copies: _____

EXHIBIT B
Form of End User License

EXHIBIT C
Training, Support and Maintenance

Training

Support

Maintenance

EXHIBIT D
Licensor Trademarks and Policy for Their Use

XX: Form 3: Marketing and Distribution Agreement

Model Exam for Final, 1999

JOINT DEVELOPMENT AND MARKETING AGREEMENT

This Joint Development and Marketing Agreement ("**Agreement**") is made and entered as of _____, 2000 ("**Effective Date**"), by and between KillerApp, Inc., a _____ corporation with offices at _____ ("**KillerApp**"), and ZoomDisk, Inc., a _____ corporation, with offices at _____ ("**Company**").

In consideration of the mutual promises contained herein and for other good and valuable consideration, the parties hereto agree as follows:

1. DEFINITIONS

1.1 "**API**" means an application program interface, which may include library routines, protocols or tools for building software applications.

1.2 "**Device Driver**" means the software that allows a computer's operating system to use Company's Storage Device, as described in **Exhibit A**.

1.3 "**Intellectual Property Rights**" means all current and future worldwide patents, patent applications, trade secrets, copyrights, copyright registrations and applications therefor, and all other intellectual property rights and proprietary rights (except trademarks, trade dress, service marks and related rights), whether arising under the laws of the United States of America, or any other state, country or jurisdiction.

1.4 "**Interface**" means the product developed by KillerApp and Company hereunder, to allow interaction between the KillerApp Product and the Device Driver, as described in **Exhibit B**.

1.5 "**Joint Invention**" means any code, idea, design, concept, technique, method, discovery or improvement, whether or not patentable, that is conceived or reduced to practice by one or more of the inventing party's employees with one or more of the other party's employees, during the term and in the performance of this Agreement.

1.6 "**KillerApp Product**" means the software product of KillerApp, as described in **Exhibit A**.

1.9 "**Milestone**" means a progress point to be completed in the development of the Interface, as identified in the Statement of Work.

1.8 "**Net Sales**" means any and all royalties, fees, or other amounts invoiced by a party and recorded according to generally accepted accounting practices in connection with the sale, distribution, or sublicensing of a product to third parties, less, to the extent included therein: (i) credits for actual returns or amounts attributable to bad debt; (ii) amounts for shipping and handling, insurance, sales tax, or other applicable taxes; and (iii) trade discounts. In bundled transactions involving more than one product, Net Sales will be calculated by prorating Net Sales as described above, according to the wholesale list prices of the applicable products. In no event will Net Sales of the Interface be less than _____% of Net Sales for any bundled transaction. Net Sales will not include any fees for support, maintenance, or updates unless received within 90 days after the date of invoice for the initial license fee.

1.9 "**Product Release Date**" means the date the Interface is first made generally commercially available.

1.10 "**Source Materials**" means documented (determined in accordance with prevailing industry standards), human-readable and machine-readable source code in printed form and on appropriate media, including without limitation header files, make files, specialized include files, and anything else reasonably necessary to compile, build and run a software product. "Source Materials" also include applicable architectural and functional specifications and block diagrams explaining the operation of the software.

1.11 "**Statement of Work**" means the statement of work attached as **Exhibit B**.

1.12 **"Storage Device"** means the disk drives marketed by Company, as described in **Exhibit A**.

2. DEVELOPMENT AND DELIVERY OBLIGATIONS

2.1 **Statement of Work.** Each party shall complete its respective obligations described in the Statement of Work, as follows: the party listed in the "Responsible Party" column shall perform the associated Milestone, or deliver any specified deliverable ("**Deliverable**") to the other party, by the date listed in the "Due Date" column for that Deliverable.

2.2 **Deliverables of Company.** Any Milestone for which a party ("**Delivering Party**") is identified as "Responsible Party" in the Statement of Work will be deemed complete upon acceptance by other party ("**Receiving Party**"), as follows: Receiving Party shall review the Milestone or Deliverable promptly upon (a) delivery of the Deliverable by Delivering Party; or (b) notice by the Delivering Party that the Milestone is complete. Receiving Party's refusal to accept a Milestone or Deliverable must be reasonable, must be in writing and must be accompanied by reasons given in sufficient detail that deficiencies can be rectified. Any Milestone or Deliverable will be deemed accepted if Delivering Party has not received from Receiving Party notification of rejection of the Milestone or Deliverable within 10 days after delivery.

2.3 **Costs.** Unless otherwise agreed in writing, the parties will each be responsible for development costs incurred by such party in its activities under this Section 2, and each party shall obtain or secure the use of any equipment and resources as may be necessary for the performance of such party's activities under this Section 2.

2.4 **Remedies.** In the event the Product Release Date has not occurred by _____, either party may terminate this Agreement; provided however, that such termination may not take place once the Product Release Date occurs. Such termination will be each party's sole remedy and sole liability for failure to complete the development of the Interface under this Section 2.

3. MARKETING AND FEES

3.1 **Marketing and Promotion.** Each party shall cooperate with other party in marketing and promoting the Interface to customers, including, but not limited to: making joint sales calls, cooperating at trade shows, and collaborating in joint press releases, **[as described in Exhibit C]**.

3.2 **Royalties.** No later than 30 days after the end of each calendar quarter, each party shall pay to the other party a royalty of 5% of Net Sales of the Interface received by such party during such quarter.

3.3 **Commissions.** No later than 30 days after the end of each calendar quarter, each party shall pay to the other party a royalty of 5% of Net Sales received by such party during such quarter as a result of referrals by the other party for sales of all products other than the Interface.

3.4 **Payment Terms.** All payments hereunder exclude all sales, use, and other taxes that may be imposed upon such payments. In the event of a late payment, the party to whom the payment was due may, in addition to any other remedies it may have, charge a late fee of 1% per month, or the maximum rate allowed under law, whichever is less, for any unpaid balance.

3.5 **Audit.** Each party shall maintain complete and accurate books and records with respect to copies and distribution of the Interface, or otherwise pertaining to the payment of fees hereunder, until at least 3 years after the applicable report and payment under this Section 3. The other party or its agent (a certified public accountant) may at any time, on at least 10 business days prior notice, audit the books and records of such party pertaining to the payment of fees hereunder. Any such audit must be performed at the requesting party's expense during normal business hours and subject to such agent's agreement to comply with confidentiality obligations substantially equivalent to those in Section 8 below. If, however, such audit reveals an underpayment of 5% or more of the amount that should have been paid for the period audited, then the underpaying party shall pay, in addition to all amounts due, the reasonable costs of such audit.

4. OWNERSHIP RIGHTS

4.1 **KillerApp Product** As between the parties, KillerApp will retain all right, title and interest, including all Intellectual Property Rights, in and to the KillerApp Product.

4.2 **Storage Device and Device Driver.** As between the parties, Company will retain all right, title and interest, including all Intellectual Property Rights, in and to the Storage Device and Device Driver.

4.3 **Interface.** The Interface will be jointly owned by the parties. Each party hereby assigns and shall assign to other party an undivided one-half interest in the Interface and all Intellectual Property Rights therein. Each party may exploit the Interface without reporting to or paying royalties to the other party, except as required by this Agreement.

4.4 **Further Assurances**. Each party shall, and shall cause its employees and agents to, sign, execute and acknowledge or cause to be signed, executed and acknowledged without costs at the expense of the other party, any and all documents and perform such acts as may be reasonably requested by the other party for the purposes of perfecting the foregoing assignments and obtaining, enforcing and defending the Intellectual Property Rights related thereto.

5. LICENSE GRANTS

5.1 **Development Licenses**

(a) KillerApp hereby grants to Company a worldwide, non-exclusive, non-transferable, royalty-free license, during the term of this Agreement prior to the Product Release Date, to use and to prepare derivative works of the Source Materials for the KillerApp Product, solely to perform Company's development obligations under Section 2.

(b) Company hereby grants to KillerApp a worldwide, non-exclusive, non-transferable, royalty-free license, during the term of this Agreement prior to the Product Release Date, to use and to prepare derivative works of the Source Materials for the Device Driver, solely to perform KillerApp's development obligations under Section 2.

5.2 **Reservation of Rights**. Each party shall not cause or permit reverse engineering, disassembly or decompilation of other party's materials to the extent such materials are provided in object code format. Each party hereby reserves all rights not expressly granted herein.

6. TRADEMARKS

6.1 **Trademark License**. Each party hereby ("**Licensor**") grants to the other party ("**Licensee**") during the term of this Agreement the right to use the trademarks, trade names and logos of the other party ("**Trademarks**"), solely to exercise its rights or to perform its obligations under this Agreement.

6.2 **Restrictions**. Except as set forth in this Section 6, nothing contained in this Agreement will be deemed to grant to Licensee any right, title or interest in or to Licensor's Trademarks. Licensee shall not, at any time during or after the term of this Agreement, challenge or assist others to challenge Licensor's Trademarks, or the registration thereof, or attempt to register any trademarks, marks or trade names confusingly similar to those of the other party.

7. TERM AND TERMINATION

7.1 **Term**. This Agreement will commence on the Effective Date and will continue for 3 years after the Product Release Date, unless earlier terminated under this Section 7.

7.2 **Automatic Termination**. Either party may terminate this Agreement upon written notice to other if and when the other party admits in writing to its inability to pay its debts in ordinary course of business as due, or makes assignment for benefit of creditors, or ceases business in ordinary course.

7.3 **Termination for Cause**. Either party may terminate this Agreement upon written notice to other upon occurrence of any material breach hereof by the other party, if the breaching party has not cured such breach for a period of 30 days after receipt of written notice from the non-breaching party.

7.4 **Survival**. The obligations in the following Sections will survive any expiration or termination of this Agreement: 1, 3.5, 4, 5.2, 6.2, 7.4, 7.5, 8, 9, 10, and 11. Sections 3.1 through 3.4 will survive as to any payment obligations accruing before: (a) the date 3 years after the Effective Date, if this Agreement is terminated after the Product Release Date; or (b) the effective date of termination, if this Agreement is terminated before the Product Release Date. All other obligations will terminate upon the effective date of termination.

7.5 **LIMITATION OF LIABILITY.** EXCEPT FOR LIABILITY FOR THIRD PARTY CLAIMS ARISING OUT OF SECTION 10, NEITHER PARTY WILL BE LIABLE TO THE OTHER FOR ANY INDIRECT, INCIDENTAL, SPECIAL OR CONSEQUENTIAL DAMAGES, OR DAMAGES FOR LOSS OF PROFITS, REVENUE, DATA, OR USE, INCURRED BY EITHER PARTY OR ANY THIRD PARTY, WHETHER IN AN ACTION IN CONTRACT OR IN TORT, EVEN IF SUCH PARTY HAS BEEN ADVISED OF THE POSSIBILITY OF SUCH DAMAGES.

8. CONFIDENTIALITY

8.1 **"Confidential Information"** means any proprietary information of a party to this Agreement, disclosed by one party to other, prior to date of this Agreement but related to subject matter hereof, or during the term of this Agreement. Confidential Information of each party will include without limitation any Source Materials or APIs provided by such party hereunder.**[Note: This means disclosure of the Source Materials for the Interface will be restricted for both parties.]**

8.2 **Exceptions**. Confidential Information will not include any information which: (i) was publicly known and made generally available prior to the time of disclosure by the disclosing party; (ii) becomes publicly known and made generally available after disclosure by disclosing party to receiving party; (iii) is already in the possession of receiving party at the time of disclosure; (iv) is obtained by receiving party from a third party without a breach of such third party's obligations of confidentiality; (v) is independently developed by receiving party without use of or reference to disclosing party's Confidential Information; or (vi) is required by law to be disclosed by receiving party, provided that receiving party gives disclosing party advance notice thereof to enable disclosing party to seek a protective order or otherwise prevent such disclosure.

8.3 **Non-Disclosure and Non-Use**. Each party: (a) shall not use any Confidential Information of the other party except for the purpose of exercising its rights and performing its obligations under this Agreement; and (b) shall not disclose such Confidential Information to any third party, except on a "need to know" basis to persons or entities that have signed a non-disclosure agreement containing substantially the terms of Sections 8.1, 8.2 and 8.3.

8.4 **Additional Responsibilities**. Each party shall either confirm the existence of, or obtain the execution of, confidentiality agreements (at least as protective as this Agreement) with its employees and contractors having access to Confidential Information of the other party.

8.5 **Confidentiality and Press Release**. Each party shall not disclose any terms of this Agreement to any third party without the consent of the other party, except as required by securities or other applicable laws, or as disclosed to prospective investors or such party's accountants, attorneys and other professional advisors, provided such parties are acting under a duty of confidentiality. Notwithstanding the above, the parties shall issue a mutually acceptable press release regarding the development of the Interface no later than __ days after the Effective Date.

9. REPRESENTATIONS AND WARRANTIES

9.1 **Authority**. Each party hereby represents and warrants to the other that: (a) such party has the right, power and authority to enter into this Agreement and to fully perform all of its obligations hereunder; and (b) entering into this Agreement does not and will not violate any agreement or obligation existing between such party and any third party.

9.2 **Intellectual Property Warranties.** Each party hereby represents and warrants to the other party that the information, Intellectual Property Rights, and materials it provides hereunder do not and will not, to the best of such party's knowledge, infringe any third party's Intellectual Property Rights.

9.3 **Disclaimer**. EXCEPT FOR THE WARRANTIES IN THIS SECTION 9, EACH PARTY HEREBY DISCLAIMS ANY AND ALL WARRANTIES, EXPRESS, IMPLIED, STATUTORY OR OTHERWISE, INCLUDING WITHOUT LIMITATION ANY IMPLIED WARRANTIES OF MERCHANTABILITY AND FITNESS FOR A PARTICULAR PURPOSE.

10. INDEMNIFICATION

10.1 **Mutual Indemnity**. Each party ("**Indemnifying Party**") shall, at its own expense, defend or at its option settle any claim brought against the other party (the "**Indemnified Party**") or its employees, directors, distributors, agents, customers, licensees, successors and assigns, and pay any associated third-party damages, expenses or settlements arising out of any breach of any warranty made by the Indemnifying Party under Section 9; or the alleged infringement or misappropriation of any third-party Intellectual Property Right by the materials provided by such party hereunder (which, in the case of KillerApp, means the KillerApp Product, and in the case of Company, means the Device Driver and Storage Device) (**"Indemnified Materials"**). THE FOREGOING PROVISIONS OF THIS SECTION 10.1 STATE THE ENTIRE LIABILITY AND OBLIGATIONS OF EACH PARTY, AND THE EXCLUSIVE REMEDY OF EACH PARTY, WITH RESPECT TO ANY ACTUAL OR ALLEGED INFRINGEMENT OF ANY INTELLECTUAL PROPERTY RIGHT.

10.2 **Limitation**. The Indemnifying Party will have no obligation with respect to any claim under Section 10.1 unless: (a) such Indemnifying Party is promptly notified of such claim; (b) the Indemnified Party allows the Indemnifying Party sole control of the defense and settlement of such claim; and (c) the Indemnified Party provides the Indemnifying Party with reasonable assistance, at the Indemnifying Party's expense, in connection with the Indemnifying Party's defense and settlement of such claim.

10.3 **Additional Intellectual Property Remedy**. If the Indemnified Materials infringe or misappropriate, or in the reasonable determination of the Indemnifying Party, are likely to infringe or misappropriate, any third party's Intellectual Property Rights, then the Indemnifying Party may, at its sole option and expense: (a) obtain from such third party the right to continue to use the Indemnified Materials consistent with the rights granted hereunder; or (b) modify the Indemnified Materials to avoid and eliminate such infringement or misappropriation.

11. GENERAL PROVISIONS

11.1 **Independent Contractors**. The relationship of KillerApp and Company established by the Agreement is that of independent contractors, and nothing contained in this Agreement will be construed to: (a) give either party the power to direct and control the day-to-day activities of the other; (b) constitute the parties as partners, joint ventures, co-owners or otherwise as participants in a joint or common undertaking; or (c) allow either party to create or assume any obligation on behalf of the other party.

11.2 **Arbitration and Governing Law**. This Agreement will be construed under the laws of the State of California, excluding its conflict of laws principles. In the event a dispute arises between the parties hereto arising out of this Agreement or any breach thereof, such dispute must be determined and settled by binding arbitration in **[San Francisco, California]**, in accordance with the rules of the American Arbitration Association.

11.3 **Notices**. Any notice or other communication required or permitted hereunder must be in writing and must be sent by reasonable means to the address of the recipient party first written above. Such notice will be deemed to have been given when delivered, or, if delivery is not accomplished by some fault of the addressee, when tendered.

11.4 **Nonassignability and Binding Effect**. Neither party may assign or delegate this Agreement or any of its licenses, rights or duties under this Agreement without prior written consent of the other party. Notwithstanding the foregoing, either party may assign this Agreement without consent of the other party: (a) to an entity into which it has merged or which has otherwise succeeded to all or substantially all of its business, stock, or assets, and which has assumed in writing its obligations under this Agreement; and (b) provided that if such an assignment occurs before the Product Release Date, the other party may terminate this Agreement by written notice at any time prior to the Product Release Date. Any attempted assignment in violation of this Section 11.4 will be void.

11.5 **Severability**. If any provision of this Agreement is held to be invalid, unlawful or unenforceable, such provision or part will be severed from this Agreement, and the remainder of the provisions, terms and conditions of this Agreement will continue to be valid and enforceable. The parties shall make reasonable, good faith efforts to amend any severed provision or part of this Agreement so as to preserve the intentions of the Agreement as much as possible.

11.6 **Integration**. This Agreement, including the Statement of Work and any other Exhibits hereto, constitutes the entire agreement between KillerApp and Company and supersedes all prior or contemporaneous agreements or representations, written or oral, concerning the subject matter of this Agreement. This Agreement may not be modified or amended except in writing and signed by a duly authorized representative of each party to this Agreement.

11.7 **Waiver**. No waiver of any term or condition of this Agreement will be valid or binding on either party unless the same is mutually assented to in writing by an officer of both parties. The failure of either party to enforce at any time any of the provisions of this Agreement, or the failure to require at any time performance by the other party of any of the provisions of this Agreement, will in no way be construed to be a present of future waiver of such provisions, nor in any way affect the validity of either party to enforce each and every such provision thereafter.

11.8 **Force Majeure**. Neither party will be liable to the other party for any loss or damage resulting from any delay or failure to perform all or any part of this if such delay or failure is caused, in whole or in party, by circumstances, beyond the control and without negligence of the party. Such circumstances include without limitation, acts of God, strikes, lockouts, riots, acts of war, acts of deadly violence, earthquakes, floods, fire and explosions.

The parties have signed below to indicate their acceptance of the terms of this Agreement.

KILLERAPP, INC.	"COMPANY"
By:_____	By:_____
Name:_____	Name:_____
Title:_____	Title:_____

EXHIBIT A
PRODUCTS

[Describe Device Driver]
[Describe KillerApp Software]
[Describe Storage Device]

EXHIBIT B

STATEMENT OF WORK

NOTES

XXI: Form 4: "Co-Branding" Agreement

Model Exam for Fall, 2000

Virtual Makeover System License Agreement

This Virtual Makeover System License Agreement ("**Agreement**") is made as of January 1, 2000 ("**Effective Date**"), by and among HairWizard[**, Inc.**], a California corporation with offices at _____ ("**HairWizard**"); General Petroleum[**, Inc.**], a Delaware corporation with offices at _____; and Heavy-2-O[**, Inc.**], a wholly-owned subsidiary of General Petroleum that is a New York corporation with offices at _____ ("**H2O**").

WHEREAS, HairWizard has developed a virtual makeover system that allows web users to superimpose images of various hair styles and hair colors on a user-provided photo; and

WHEREAS, H2O markets and sells hair care products containing "heavy oil," which is a form of petroleum supersaturated with sea minerals that is a useable by-product of oil spills; and

WHEREAS, the Parties desire users of H2O's e-commerce web site to be able to use HairWizard's virtual makeover system, in order to promote the sales of H2O's hair care products.

NOW, THEREFORE, the Parties agree as follows:

1. DEFINITIONS

1.1 "**Advertising Revenue**" means any fees invoiced by H2O in connection with the appearance of banner advertisements, buttons, tiles, text promotions, and the like on any page on the H2O Web Site containing any portion of the Virtual Makeover System. In the event H2O accepts any non-monetary consideration for any such advertising, Advertising Revenue will also include the fair market value of such advertisements. In the event that amounts are invoiced for advertising appearing on such pages and also on other pages on the H2O Web Site, a portion of such amounts, prorated based on the number of impressions on such pages and such other pages, will be included in Advertising Revenue.

1.2 "**H2O Developed Information**" means information regarding users of the H2O Web Site that is not entered by the user, but prepared by H2O, including without limitation cookies, user traffic data, preferences, and user transactional history, as described in Section 10.5(b).

1.3 "**H2O Web Site**" means the Web Site operated by H2O available at the URL www.heavy-2-o.com, and any mirror, satellite, or replacement sites thereof operated by or for H2O during the term of this Agreement.

1.4 "**HairWizard Content**" means any picture, image, figure, graphical material, videos, charts, writings, or other text and any other materials (other than software) provided to H2O by HairWizard as part of the Virtual Makeover System.

1.5 "**HairWizard Web Site**" means the Web Site operated by HairWizard available at the URL www.hairwizard.com.

1.6 "**Launch**" means to make the H2O Web Site, in a form that includes the e-commerce functionality described in Exhibit B, as well as the Virtual Makeover System, generally available on the World Wide Web.

1.7 A "**Party**" means HairWizard or H2O. "**Parties**" means HairWizard or H2O.

1.8 "**Product Revenue**" means any fees invoiced by H2O in connection with the sales of goods or services to any user that has viewed, in the current viewing session, any page of the H2O Web Site containing any portion of the Virtual Makeover System; less only, to the extent included therein, freight, sales tax, and insurance.

1.9 "**Registration Information**" means any personal information provided by users of the H2O Web Site, including without limitation contact name, address, email address, telephone number, and demographic information.

1.10 **"Service Standards"** means the service guidelines attached as Exhibit C which describe the minimum standards for speed, and traffic capacity for the H2O Web Site.

1.11 **"Software"** means any computer software code provided to H2O by HairWizard as part of the Virtual Makeover System, in object code format, along with any updates, patches or new versions thereof provided by HairWizard hereunder.

1.12 **"Virtual Makeover System"** means HairWizard's system that allows a Web Site user to superimpose different hair styles and hair colors on a user-supplied photo, in substantially the form available on the HairWizard Web Site, as described in Exhibit A. The Virtual Makeover System includes the HairWizard Content and the Software.

1.13 **"Web Site"** means a set of HTML-based compilations of integrated content or other materials, which may, through software known as a browser, be displayed on a user's computers by means of a download to local cache memory, using the HTTP protocol service of the Internet.

2. DELIVERY AND IMPLEMENTATION OF VIRTUAL MAKEOVER SYSTEM

2.1 **Delivery**. On or before the Effective Date, HairWizard shall deliver to H2O, by electronic means or on magnetic or optical media, one copy of the Virtual Makeover System.

2.2 **Support**. HairWizard shall provide second-tier technical support services **[by telephone, fax-back and e-mail]** to H2O's technical support staff during HairWizard's regular business hours regarding the operation of the Virtual Makeover System. HairWizard will not be obligated to provide technical support to users of the H2O Web Site.

2.3 **Launch and Service Standards**. H2O shall Launch the H2O Web Site on or before January 1, 2001.

2.4 **Hypertext Links**. HairWizard shall place, on the top-level home page of HairWizard Web Site, a link to the H2O Web Site. Such placement must be as shown in Exhibit D. H2O shall place, on the top-level home page of H2O Web Site, a link to the HairWizard Web Site. Such placement must be as shown in Exhibit E. H2O shall also place, on every page of the H2O Web Site containing any portion of the HairWizard Virtual Makeover System, the legend "Powered by HairWizard" and a reasonably prominent link to the HairWizard Web Site.

2.5 **Software Updates**. HairWizard shall provide H2O with any updates or new versions of the Virtual Makeover System on or before the date such updates or new versions are deployed on the HairWizard Web Site. H2O shall at all times use on the H2O Web Site only the latest version of the Software provided by HairWizard.

3. EXCLUSIVITY

3.1 **H2O's Obligation**. H2O shall not use any virtual makeover system other than the Virtual Makeover System on the H2O Web Site.

3.2 **HairWizard's Obligation**. HairWizard shall not place advertising for any **[hair care]** products on the HairWizard Web Site other than H2O hair care products. However, if the total amounts received by HairWizard from H2O hereunder as of January 31, 2002 are less than $500,000, the foregoing obligation will automatically cease in effect.

3.3 **Press Release.** Notwithstanding the provisions of Section 10.7, the Parties shall issue a mutually acceptable press release regarding the use of the Virtual Makeover System on the H2O Web Site on or before the Launch.

4. GRANT OF LICENSES

4.1 **Content**. Subject to the terms and conditions of this Agreement, HairWizard hereby grants to H2O a non-exclusive, non-transferable, non-sublicenseable, worldwide license during the term of this Agreement:

(a) to use the HairWizard Content and derivative works thereof, solely in connection with the operation of the Virtual Makeover System on the H2O Web Site;

(b) to prepare derivative works of the HairWizard Content, solely in connection with the operation of the Virtual Makeover System on the H2O Web Site, and provided that all modifications to the HairWizard Content other than changes in size must be approved in advance in writing by HairWizard, such approval not to be unreasonably withheld;

(c) to reproduce and distribute the HairWizard Content, solely as necessary to exercise the rights granted in clauses (a) and (b).

4.2 **Software**. Subject to the terms and conditions of this Agreement, HairWizard hereby grants to H2O a non-exclusive, non-transferable, non-sublicenseable, worldwide license during the term of this Agreement:

(a) to use the Software on the computer server hosting the H2O Web Site, or on a backup server if the primary server is not functioning;

(b) to reproduce the Software solely as necessary to exercise the rights granted under Section 2.2(a), and to make a reasonable number of archival copies of the Software.

4.3 **Trademarks**

(a) **License**. During the term of this Agreement, each Party ("Licensor") grants to the other Party ("Licensee") the right to display the trademarks, marks and trade names that Licensor may adopt from time to time ("Marks") on Licensee's Web Site, solely as necessary to perform Licensee's obligations under this Agreement. Prior to such display, Licensee shall submit to Licensor all representations of the Marks that Licensee intends to use in connection with the foregoing license, for Licensor's approval of design, color, and other details. Licensee shall display such Marks only in accordance with any guidelines for the use of such Marks provided by Licensor from time to time.

(b) **Assignment of Goodwill**. If Licensee, in the course of performing its services hereunder, acquires any goodwill or reputation in any of the Marks, all such goodwill or reputation will automatically vest in Licensor when and as, on an on-going basis, such acquisition of goodwill or reputation occurs, as well as at the expiration or termination of this Agreement, without any separate payment or other consideration of any kind to Licensee, and Licensee shall take all such actions necessary to effect such vesting. Licensee shall not contest the validity of any of the Marks or Licensor's exclusive ownership of them. During the term of this Agreement, Licensee shall not adopt, use, or register, whether as a corporate name, trademark, service mark or other indication of origin, any of the Marks, or any word or mark confusingly similar to them in any jurisdiction.

4.4 **Reverse Engineering**. H2O shall not reverse engineer, disassemble, decompile, or otherwise attempt to derive the source code of the Software.

4.5 **Ownership**

(a) **Content**. As between H2O and HairWizard, HairWizard will retain ownership of the HairWizard Content and all intellectual property rights therein.

(b) **Software**. As between H2O and HairWizard, HairWizard will retain ownership of the Software and all intellectual property rights therein.

5. FEES AND PAYMENTS

5.1 **Payments**. All payments must be made in U.S. dollars, and must be accompanied by a report in reasonable detail showing the basis for such payments.

5.2 **Advertising Revenue**. No later than 30 days after the end of each calendar month during the term of this Agreement, H2O shall pay HairWizard 50% of all Advertising Revenues invoiced for such month.

5.3 **Product Sales**. No later than 30 days after the end of each calendar month during the term of this Agreement, H2O shall pay HairWizard 5% of all Product Sales for such month.

5.4 **Audits**. H2O shall keep and maintain complete and accurate records of the transactions underlying the accounting statements to be furnished under this Section 5, and shall allow HairWizard, or its representative, during office hours and no more than once every six months, to inspect and make extracts or copies of such records solely for the purpose of ascertaining the correctness of such statements. If any such audit shall discloses any deficiency of 5% or more, H2O shall pay, in addition to such deficiency, the costs of such audit.

6. TERM AND TERMINATION

6.1 **Term**. This Agreement will remain in force commencing on the Effective Date and continuing for a period of 36 months, unless earlier terminated in accordance with this Section 6. Upon the expiration of such 36-month period, this Agreement will continue in effect indefinitely until terminated by either Party upon no less than 30 days prior written notice.

6.2 **Default**. If either Party materially defaults in the performance of any of its material obligations hereunder and if any such default is not corrected within 30 days after notice in writing, then the non-defaulting Party, at its option, may, in addition to any other remedies it may have, thereupon terminate this Agreement by giving written notice of termination to the defaulting Party.

6.3 **Failure to Launch**. If the Launch has not occurred by _____, either Party may terminate this Agreement upon written notice. After the Launch occurs, the provisions of this Section 6.3 will cease in effect.

6.4 **Insolvency**. Either Party may terminate this Agreement upon written notice: (a) upon the other Party's insolvency, initiation of receivership or bankruptcy proceedings or any other proceeding for the settlement of its debts; (b) upon the initiation of such proceedings against the other Party, which are not dismissed within 60 days thereafter; (c) upon the other Party's making a general assignment for the benefit of creditors; or (d) upon the other Party's dissolution or ceasing to conduct business in the ordinary course.

6.5 **Survival**. The rights and obligations of the following Sections will survive any expiration or termination of this Agreement: 1 (Definitions), 4 (Ownership), 5.4 (Audits), 7 (Representations and Warranties), 8 (Indemnities), 9 (Limitation of Liability), 10 (Confidentiality) and 11 (Miscellaneous). Section 5 (Fees and Payments) will survive as to any payment obligations accruing before the date of termination.

7. REPRESENTATIONS AND WARRANTIES

7.1 **General Warranties**. Each Party hereby represents and warrants that:

(a) it has the right to enter into this Agreement; it is a corporation duly organized, validly existing, and in good standing under the laws of the state of its incorporation; it has the corporate power and authority for, and has by all necessary corporate action authorized, the execution and delivery of this Agreement, and the performance of its obligations hereunder; and

(b) the execution, performance and delivery of this Agreement by such Party will not conflict with or violate or result in any breach of, or constitute a default under, any contract, agreement or other obligation of such Party.

7.2 **Software Performance**. HairWizard represents and warrants to H2O that during the term of this Agreement, the Software will perform substantially as set forth in the specifications in Exhibit A. HairWizard's sole liability and H2O's sole remedy with respect to such warranty will be HairWizard's obligation to use commercially reasonable efforts to correct, within a reasonable period of time, any documented and reproducible defects in the Software that cause the Software not to perform in all material respects in accordance with the specifications in Exhibit A.

7.3 **Exclusions**. The warranty under Section 7.2 will not extend to problems that result from: (i) H2O failure to implement all updates, patches and new revisions of the Software delivered to H2O by HairWizard; (ii) changes to the operating system of physical, hardware or software environment which adversely affect the Software; (iii) any alterations of or additions to the Software or HairWizard Content performed by parties other than HairWizard; (iv) accident or misuse of the Software; or (v) use of the Software on equipment not approved by HairWizard.

7.3 **Intellectual Property Warranty**. HairWizard hereby represents and warrants to H2O that the Virtual Makeover System and the use thereof as allowed under this Agreement does not and will not infringe any third party's copyright or trade secret rights. HairWizard hereby represents and warrants to H2O that, to the best of HairWizard's knowledge as of the Effective Date, the Virtual Makeover System and the use thereof as allowed under this Agreement does not infringe any third party's patent or trademark rights.

7.4 **Disclaimer**. EXCEPT FOR THE WARRANTIES EXPRESSED IN THIS SECTION 7, EACH PARTY DISCLAIMS ANY AND ALL WARRANTIES, EXPRESS, IMPLIED, STATUTORY OR OTHERWISE, INCLUDING WITHOUT LIMITATION ANY IMPLIED WARRANTIES OF MERCHANTABILITY, FITNESS FOR A PARTICULAR PURPOSE, AND NON-INFRINGEMENT.

8. INDEMNITIES

8.1 **Indemnity**. Each Party shall, at its own expense, defend or at its option settle any claim brought against the other Party to the extent that such claims arise out of any breach of any warranty made by such Party under Section 7, provided that the other Party provides such Party with: (i) prompt written notice of such claim; (ii) control over the defense and settlement of such claim; and (iii) information and assistance to settle or defend any such claim. Such indemnity shall be each Party's sole remedy for such breach of warranty.

8.2 **HairWizard's Options**. Should the Virtual Makeover System or any portion thereof become, or in HairWizard's opinion be likely to become, the subject of any infringement claim or suit, HairWizard may, at its option: (i) procure for H2O the right to continue using the infringing material, pursuant to the rights granted in this Agreement; or (ii) modify such material such that it no longer infringes the proprietary rights of any third party, provided that any modifications to the Software must not result in loss of functionality of the Software.

8.3 **Exclusive Remedy**. THE FOREGOING PROVISIONS OF THIS SECTION 8 STATE THE ENTIRE LIABILITY AND OBLIGATIONS OF EACH PARTY, AND THE EXCLUSIVE REMEDY OF EACH PARTY, WITH RESPECT TO ANY ACTUAL OR ALLEGED INFRINGEMENT OF ANY INTELLECTUAL PROPERTY RIGHT.

9. LIMITATION OF LIABILITY

EXCEPT FOR LIABILITY UNDER SECTION 10 (CONFIDENTIALITY), NEITHER PARTY WILL BE LIABLE TO THE OTHER FOR ANY INDIRECT, INCIDENTAL, SPECIAL OR CONSEQUENTIAL DAMAGES, OR DAMAGES FOR LOSS OF PROFITS, REVENUE, DATA, OR USE, INCURRED BY EITHER PARTY OR ANY THIRD PARTY, WHETHER IN AN ACTION IN CONTRACT OR IN TORT, EVEN IF SUCH PARTY HAS BEEN ADVISED OF THE POSSIBILITY OF SUCH DAMAGES. EXCEPT FOR LIABILITY FOR THIRD PARTY CLAIMS ARISING OUT OF SECTION 8 (INDEMNITIES), NEITHER PARTY'S AGGREGATE LIABILITY FOR DAMAGES HEREUNDER WILL IN ANY EVENT EXCEED THE AMOUNT OF FEES PAID BY H2O TO HAIRWIZARD UNDER THIS AGREEMENT.

10. CONFIDENTIALITY

10.1 "**Confidential Information**" means any proprietary information of a Party to this Agreement disclosed to the other Party hereunder, including, without limitation, any such information related to the Virtual Makeover System, research, customer lists, marketing information, finance information or other business information.

10.2 **Exceptions**. Confidential Information will not include any information that (i) was publicly known and made generally available prior to the time of disclosure by the disclosing Party; (ii) becomes publicly known and made generally available after disclosure by the disclosing Party to the receiving Party through no action or inaction of the receiving Party; (iii) is already in the possession of the receiving Party at the time of disclosure; (iv) is obtained by the receiving Party from a third party without a breach of such third party's obligations of confidentiality; (v) is independently developed by the receiving Party without use of or reference to the disclosing Party's Confidential Information; or (vi) is required by law to be disclosed by the receiving Party, provided that the receiving Party gives the disclosing Party prompt written notice of such requirement prior to such disclosure and assistance in obtaining an order protecting the information from public disclosure.

10.3 **Non-Disclosure and Non-Use**. Each Party: (a) shall treat as confidential all Confidential Information of the other Party; (b) shall not disclose such Confidential Information to any third party, except on a "need to know" basis to third parties that have signed a non-disclosure agreement containing substantially the terms of Sections 10.1 and 10.2 and this Section 10.3; and (c) shall not use such Confidential Information except in connection with performing its obligations or exercising its rights under this Agreement.

10.4 **Return of Materials** All documents and other tangible objects containing or representing Confidential Information to which have been disclosed by either Party to the other Party, and all copies thereof which are in the possession of the other Party, will remain the property of the disclosing Party and must be promptly returned to the disclosing Party upon the disclosing Party's written request.

10.5 **Customer and Web Site Information**

(a) **Registration Information**. The Parties acknowledge that H2O will collect certain Registration Information from users of the H2O Web Site. This sub-Section 10.5(a), and not the foregoing provisions of this Section 10, will apply to any Registration Information. Neither Party shall disclose any Registration Information to any third party in individually identifiable form. For purposes of the foregoing, "individually identifiable form" (a) includes disclosure in a form where an individual datum that is unique to a user is disclosed, such as in the distribution of customer lists or email lists; and (b) does not include the disclosure of data aggregated in such a way that a certain user's registration information can not be determined using reasonable efforts. Each Party may use Registration Information to promote, develop, or enhance the H2O Web Site or HairWizard Web Site, subject to any privacy policy appearing on the H2O Web Site, however, neither Party shall use the Registration Information to conduct direct mail, e-mail, or similar solicitations unless the other Party agrees in advance in writing, including approval of the content any such solicitation.

(b) **Developed Information**. The Parties acknowledge that H2O will develop the H2O Developed Information. This sub-Section 10.5(b), and not the foregoing provisions of this Section 10, will apply to Developed Information. Each Party may use the H2O Developed Information for any purpose and may disclose such information to third parties in its sole discretion, subject to any privacy policy appearing on the H2O Web Site.

(c) **Non-Disclosure of Customer Relationship**. Without limiting the above provisions of this Section 10, during the term of this Agreement and for a period of 12 months thereafter, neither Party shall disclose to any direct competitor of the other

Party any Registration Information or individually identifiable Developed Information. The Parties acknowledge that such restriction is necessary to protect the value of each Party's proprietary information.

(d) **Confidentiality of Agreement**. Neither Party shall disclose the terms of this Agreement to any third party without the consent of the other Party, except as required by securities or other applicable laws. Notwithstanding the previous sentence, a Party may disclose the terms of this Agreement to its accountants, attorneys or to potential investors in connection with a proposed merger, acquisition, investment, or asset sale, so long as such parties are acting under a duty of confidentiality.

11. MISCELLANEOUS

11.1 **Arbitration and Governing Law**. The laws of the state of California, except its conflicts of law provisions, will govern this Agreement. In the event a dispute arises between the Parties arising out of this Agreement or any breach thereof, such dispute will be determined and settled by binding arbitration in **[San Francisco, California]**, in accordance with the rules of the American Arbitration Association. The award rendered thereon by the arbitrator will be final and binding on the Parties, and judgment thereon may be entered in any court of competent jurisdiction. Nothing in this Section11.1 will prevent either Party from applying to a court of competent jurisdiction for equitable or injunctive relief.

11.2 **Force Majeure**. Neither Party will be liable to the other Party for any loss or damage resulting from any delay or failure to perform all or any part of this Agreement (except failure to pay monies due) if such delay or failure is caused, in whole or in part, by circumstances beyond the control and without negligence of the Party. Such circumstances include, without limitation, acts of God, strikes, lockouts, riots, acts of war, acts of deadly violence, earthquakes, floods, fire and explosions.

11.3 **Assignment**. This Agreement will be binding upon and inure to the benefit of the Parties and their respective successors and assigns; provided, however, that neither Party shall assign any of its rights, obligations, or privileges (by operation of law or otherwise) hereunder without the prior written consent of the other Party. Notwithstanding the foregoing, either Party may assign all of its relevant assets, in connection with an asset sale, merger, or corporate reorganization. Any attempted assignment in violation of this Section 11.3 will be void.

11.4 **Severability**. If any provision or part of this Agreement is found to be invalid, unlawful or unenforceable, such provision or part will be severed from this Agreement and the remainder of the provisions, terms and conditions of this Agreement will continue to be valid and enforceable. The Parties shall use reasonable and good faith efforts to amend any severed provision or part of this Agreement so as to preserve the intentions of the Agreement as much as possible.

11.5 **Waiver**. A waiver of any provision of this Agreement or of a Party's rights or remedies under this Agreement must be in writing and signed by an authorized representative of the waiving Party to be effective. Failure, neglect or delay by a Party to enforce the provisions of this Agreement or its rights or remedies under this Agreement will not be construed or deemed to be a waiver of such Party's right to do so and will not affect the validity of all or any part of this Agreement or prejudice such Party's right to take subsequent action. Neither a waiver of any provision of this Agreement or any right or remedy hereunder, nor the exercise or enforcement of any right or remedy under this Agreement, will preclude the validity and enforceability of any other provision, right or remedy under this Agreement or that a Party is entitled to by law.

11.6 **Independent Contractors**. The relationship of the Parties under this Agreement is that of independent contractors. Neither Party will be deemed to be an employee, agent, partner or legal representative of the other for any purpose and neither will have any right, power or authority to create any obligation or responsibility on behalf of the other.

11.7 **Notices**. Any notice required or permitted under the terms of this Agreement or required by law must be in writing and must be: (a) delivered in person; (b) sent by first class registered mail, or air mail, as appropriate; or (c) sent by overnight air courier, in each case properly posted and fully prepaid to the appropriate address set forth in the preamble to this Agreement. Either Party may change its address for notice by notice to the other Party given in accordance with this Section. Notices will be considered to have been given at the time of actual delivery in person, three business days after deposit in the mail as set forth above, or one day after delivery to an overnight air courier service.

11.8 **Integration**. This Agreement (including the Exhibits hereto) contains the entire agreement of the Parties with respect to the subject matter of this Agreement and supersedes all previous communications, representations, understandings and agreements, either oral or written, between the Parties with respect to said subject matter. No terms, provisions or conditions of any purchase order, acknowledgement or other business form that either Party may use in connection with the transactions contemplated by this Agreement will have any effect on the rights, duties or obligations of the Parties under, or otherwise modify, this Agreement, regardless of any failure of a receiving Party to object to such terms, provisions or conditions. This Agreement may not be amended, except by a writing signed by both Parties.

11.9 **Counterparts**. This Agreement may be executed in counterparts, each of which so executed will be deemed to be an original and such counterparts together will constitute one and the same agreement.

11.10 **Guarantee**. General Petroleum hereby guarantees the performance by H2O of its obligations under this Agreement.

HairWizard and H2O have signed below to indicate their acceptance of the terms of this Agreement.

HAIRWIZARD[, INC.]	H2O[, INC.]
By: _____	By: _____
Name: _____	Name: _____
Title: _____	Title: _____

General Petroleum[, Inc.] has signed below to indicate its acceptance of the terms of Section 11.10.

GENERAL PETROLEUM[, INC.]

By: _____

Name: _____

Title: _____

Exhibit A

Virtual Makeover System Specifications

Exhibit B

E-Commerce Functionality for H2O Web Site

Exhibit C

Service Standards for H2O Web Site

Exhibit D

Placement of Links on HairWizard Web Site

Exhibit E

Placement of Links on H2O Web Site

Endnotes

[i] A prior version of this section was published in: A Lesson In Taxonomy: The Many Monikers of The Software Distribution Agreement, The Computer Lawyer, Vol. 16, No. 11, Nov. 1999.

[ii] The nine categories above (which may seem arbitrary because they followed prior case law as of the time the 1976 Copyright Act was passed) that require a writing for the work to be considered a "work for hire" are works that are specially ordered or commissioned: (1) for use as a contribution to a collective work, (2) as part of a motion picture or other audiovisual work, (3) as a translation, (4) as a supplementary work, (5) as a compilation, (6) as an instructional text, (7) as a test, (8) as answer material for a test, or (9) as an atlas.

[iii] Factors to consider include: (a) the hiring party's level on controlling them manner and means of production; (b) the level of skill required; (c) the source of instrumentalities and tools; (d) the location of the work; (e) the duration of the relationship between the parties; (f) whether the hiring party has the right to assign additional projects to the hired party; (g) the extent of the hired party's discretion of when and how long to work; (h) the method of payment; (i) the hired party's role in hiring and paying assistants; (j) whether the work is part of the regular business of the hiring party; (k) whether the hiring party is in business; (l) the provision of employee benefits; and (m) the tax treatment of the hired party. *CCNV v. Reid*, 490 U.S. 730 (1989).

[iv] Termination provisions apply to assignments, transfers and to non-exclusive licenses. Termination may be effected at any time during a period of five years beginning at the end of 35 years from the date of execution of the grant, regardless of any agreement to the contrary. If the transferor does not exercise his or her termination rights or fails to comply with formalities associated with termination, then the transfer remains valid.

[v] Although a discussion of antitrust law is beyond the scope of this book, take a look at the antitrust guidelines for intellectual property licensing that are promulgated by the Department of Justice. These guidelines apply to licenses of patents, copyrights, and trade secrets (but not trademarks). They provide, generally, that intellectual property licenses are assessed under a rule of reason, weighing the pro-competitive effects of the license against the anti-competitive effects of any restrictions. There is no presumption that the existence of intellectual property will imply that the owner has market power for the purposes of the antitrust analysis. The guidelines also recognize that any license—even an exclusive one—is generally pro-competitive, because it creates a possibility of market activity that the licensee would not otherwise have. The guidelines further provide for a "safe harbor" from antitrust scrutiny for licenses that meet certain requirements. You can find the guidelines at http://www.usdoj.gov/atr/public/guidelines/ipguide.htm.

[vi] It is not impossible to change object code. Some "de-compiler" programs exist that can translate object code back into source code. But the translation is imperfect, and in any case, decompilation is usually prohibited under a license agreement, as we saw in Chapter 1.

[vii] Like most of the language presented here, this is subject to interpretation. If Licensor is obligated to indemnify, Licensee can always try to join the Licensor as a party in the suit, and demand payment of attorneys fees as part of the obligation to indemnify—effectively requiring a defense from Licensor.

[viii] The best known is Fisher & Ury's *Getting to Yes*.

[ix] For more information about arbitration and mediation, see the American Arbitration Association's Web site at http://www.adr.org.

[x] The reverse triangular merger has a number of tax, accounting, and corporate governance advantages, though its implementation is very counter-intuitive. It is called triangular because it involves three entities, one of which does not survive the transaction. The party wishing to purchase ("Buyer") creates a wholly-owned subsidiary ("Newco"). All of Newco's stock is owned by Buyer. The shareholders of the company being bought ("Target") trade their shares of Target in exchange for shares of Newco. Newco is then "merged into" Target in such a fashion that Newco ceases to exist. Shares of Newco are then exchanged for shares of Buyer. At the end, Target's shareholders hold some shares of Buyer, and Buyer owns all shares of Target. Thus, Target survives as a wholly-owned subsidiary of Buyer, and Newco no longer exists. If you are wondering why Target does not simply sell all its shares directly to Buyer, you are not alone. However, such a simple transaction would forfeit the tax, accounting, and corporate governance advantages of the reverse triangular structure, and the outcome is the same.

[xi] This language specifies the method of acceptance. See U.C.C. 2-206/2-207.

[xii] See 17 U.S.C. §106—Exclusive rights under copyright do not include "use."

[xiii] This language attempts to limit the scope of the license, which under copyright law may be broader.

[xiv] See 17 U.S.C. §117—This is probably an "essential step" in using the program.

[xv] See 17 U.S.C. §106—Copyright law prohibits this even in the absence of a contract.

[xvi] See 17 U.S.C. §117—Archival copies are not infringements of the right to copy.

[xvii] See 17 U.S.C. §109—Rental is prohibited by the Computer Software Rental Act.

[xviii] See 17 U.S.C. §109—First sale doctrine, where first sale exhausts the distribution right.

[xix] The restriction is partially prohibited under E.U. law.

[xx] See 17 U.S.C. §106—Copyright law prohibits this even in the absence of a contract.

[xxi] This minimal warranty is usually included to avoid a complete lack of warranty, which may be unenforceable.

[xxii] This exclusive remedy is one of the principal reasons for the license. Exclusive remedies allowed under U.C.C. 2-719.

[xxiii] This is required by the Magnuson-Moss Warranty Act, 15 U.S.C. 167; 2301 et seq.

[xxiv] Warranties under the U.C.C. 2-314 and 2-315. Limitations allowed under U.C.C. 2-316 if language is "conspicuous."

[xxv] This is required by the Magnuson-Moss Warranty Act, 15 U.S.C. 167; 2301 et seq.

[xxvi] Limitation of liability is one of the principal reasons for the license—particularly with respect to consequential damages.

[xxvii] Failure of essential purpose of limited remedies is discussed in U.C.C. 2-719

[xxviii] This is required by the Magnuson-Moss Warranty Act, 15 U.S.C. 167; 2301 et seq.

[xxix] Federal Acquisition Regulations—in a shrink wrap agreement, the licensor does not know the identity of the licensee, which may be the government.

[xxx] Licensee is probably bound by U.S. laws regardless of this provision, but the provision may be useful to prove the licensor took steps to prevent unlawful export.

[xxxi] Governing law and jurisdiction provisions are important, particularly because licensor does not know the identity of licensee.

About the Author

Heather Meeker is an attorney in private practice at Greenberg Traurig, LLP, a leading technology law firm in Silicon Valley, and specializes in drafting and negotiating intellectual property transactions for software and other technology clients. She also serves as an adjunct professor at Hastings College of the Law, teaching a seminar in intellectual property licensing, for which this textbook was developed. Ms. Meeker has degrees from Yale College and Boalt Hall School of Law. She clerked for the United States Circuit Judge John Porfilio of the Tenth Circuit. Ms. Meeker has published numerous law review articles and practice-oriented articles in the area of law and technology, and has a special interest in open source software licensing. She also worked for many years in the entertainment and computer industries, prior to her work as an attorney.

A PRIMER ON INTELLECTUAL PROPERTY LICENSING is a compact, practical guide to one of the most dynamic and popular areas of legal practice today -- intellectual property licensing. Developed by an attorney in private practice who specializes in Silicon Valley technology licensing, this guide presents the basic rules of law you need to know for a licensing practice, along with helpful examples of contractual language, practice tips, and insights on custom and practice in the industry.

Made in the USA
Middletown, DE
01 July 2017